BEDS

— AND —

BORDERS

— FOR —

YEAR ROUND
COLOUR

Jill Cowley

Photographs by Clive Nichols

WARD LOCK

PHOTOGRAPH ACKNOWLEDGEMENTS

Cover Chenies Manor House, Buckinghamshire; **4, 5** The Old Rectory, Burghfield, Berkshire; **7** White Windows, Hampshire; **9** designer Helen Dillon; **12** Keukenhof Gardens, Holland; **15** designer Anthony Noel; **19** Glazeley Old Rectory, Shropshire; **23** Vale End, Surrey; **28** Chiffchaffs, Dorset; **30** Egglesden Hall, Durham; **31, 32** The Beth Chatto Gardens, Essex; **34** Barnsley House, Gloucestershire; **40** Cerney House, Gloucestershire; **45** designers Nuala Hancock and Mathew Bell; **49** designer Anne Waring; **51** Mottisfont Abbey, Hampshire; **53** The Old Rectory, Burghfield, Berkshire; **56** Spinners, Hampshire; **61** The Beth Chatto Gardens, Essex; **63** The Priory, Kemerton, Worcestershire; **68** The Anchorage, Kent; **70** Turn End, Buckinghamshire – designer Peter Aldington; **74–5** Lower Hall, Shropshire; **77** Glazeley Old Rectory, Shropshire; **82** Hadspen House Garden and Nursery, Somerset – designers Sandra and Nori Pope; **87** The Beth Chatto Gardens, Essex; **89** White Windows, Hampshire; **92** designer Nigel Colborn; **96** Royal Horticultural Society's Garden, Wisley, Surrey; **98** The Sir Harold Hillier Gardens and Aboretum, Hampshire; **105** Butterstream, Trim, Co. Meath, Republic of Ireland – designer Jim Reynolds; **111** The Old Rectory, Burghfield, Berkshire; **118** University Botanic Garden, Cambridge; **120** The Dower House, Gloucestershire; **124–5** University Botanic Garden, Cambridge; **131** The Beth Chatto Gardens, Essex.

A WARD LOCK BOOK

First published in the UK 1995
by Ward Lock, Wellington House, 125 Strand, London WC2R 0BB

First published in paperback 1996

A Cassell Imprint

Copyright © Text Jill Cowley 1995

Distributed in the United States by Sterling Publishing Co., Inc.
387 Park Avenue South, New York, NY 10016-8810

Distributed in Australia by Capricorn Link (Australia) Pty Ltd
2/13 Carrington Road, Castle Hill NSW 2154

A British Library Cataloguing in Publication Data block for this book may be obtained from the British Library

ISBN 0-7063-7348-0 (Hbk)
ISBN 0-7063-7576-9 (Pbk)

Typeset by Method Limited, Epping, Essex
Printed and bound in Spain

CONTENTS

CHAPTER 1

DESIGNING BEDS AND BORDERS

YOUR HOUSE WILL PLAY a major role when you are deciding how your garden should look. Whether the beds and borders are swirling and romantic or disciplined and formal will depend to a great extent on the type and style of your house and its immediate surroundings. The design of beds and borders should always be in keeping with the overall site of the garden as well as accurately reflecting your own character. Many gardeners think of the

In high summer classically planted double herbaceous borders, backed by a yew hedge, provide both colour and form.

beds and borders as isolated features in the overall picture of their home, but they have an important influence in creating what is almost a theatrical setting for the house. The design of the garden does not have to conform to a standardized pattern, but it should always fit in and harmonize with its surroundings.

Of course, no two gardens will be exactly alike, even in new estates with their comparatively small, often open-plan plots, and even when a professional garden designer is employed, which sometimes leads to a certain uniformity, with the same easy plants used every time and the same conformity applied to the design, the owner's individual taste quickly overwhelms even that, so that a garden soon finds a character of its own.

A bed is usually thought of as an island with no walls or hedges to define its outlines. A border, on the other hand, is thought to be just that – a border alongside a structure or hedge to give it a background. The gardener has to create a background for the chosen plants in a bed, but in a border the plants have to be selected to paint a picture against a fixed setting.

Most people choose to have the tallest plants, shrubs or trees at the back of the border, and to layer their plants by height as they come towards the front, and the same often goes for island beds. Experienced gardeners will let a drift of lower growing plants float back into the taller subjects and sometimes let a tall, but transparent plant, such as *Verbena bonariensis*, come right to the edge of a bed or border.

In mid-winter frost highlights the architectural quality of the herbaceous plants.

FASHION IN THE GARDEN

Fashion should really have no part in the planning of a garden, but we are all influenced by the books we read and the gardens we visit. In the 1960s and 1970s little box hedges were ripped out by the mile, as the fashion changed to more naturalistic styles. Island beds, with great drifts of informal planting, became the thing, a style epitomized by the magnificent sweeps of unusual plants in the garden at Elmstead Market in Essex, in the south of England, which was created by Beth Chatto. Too often attempts to emulate this style by less gifted gardeners led to spotty planting and unsatisfactory effects.

In the late 1980s the pendulum swung the other way, and people turned to the discipline and order of a formal style, with box edges, yew hedges and topiarized pillars and balls. In the United States, the Williamsburg Gardens, Virginia, have once again become a role model, and now many gardeners have seen the virtues of exercising a bit of discipline to control those unruly roses on their pillars and to contain the floppy grasses behind box. Some gardeners may be able to afford to buy containerized box and yew, cut into the most elaborate shapes, to place artfully in their flower borders. Those of us who have to grow our own – and it takes years to grow a good yew obelisk, although a yew hedge is reasonably quick – will probably find the fashion has changed again. Don't despair – it will return just as your topiary specimen matures.

Both these styles, the formal and the informal, can be adapted to most sorts of houses. Too formal an approach will look wrong with a modern house, however, although it looks wonderful in its true milieu – the Georgian mansion with a sweeping parkland and formal beds near the house.

Cottages and small houses can take a small amount of box edging. A yew hedge improves any garden, providing the 'bones' for its formal structure that can be overlaid with luxuriant planting in the romantic style to get the best of all possible worlds. The colourful planting will be safely below ground when winter comes, yet the dark green structures will be there to give shape to your borders and beds and to create a romantic setting for the tiny scented plants that appear above ground in midwinter.

If you have a 1930s semidetached house in a suburb, a smart townhouse in a city centre, or a house in a rural setting, it is easier to follow the typical style, but it is much more fun to turn those traditions slightly on their heads. A town house may have a lot of hard landscaping – terraces, paved walks and walls – but the borders and beds can overflow with heady plantings of roses and even wild flowers and still keep the spirit of the place.

The part your house plays in deciding the style of the beds and borders – its shape and size, whether it is modern or period – has developed with gardening history. Cottagers collected seeds and 'slips' from their master's gardens and planted them haphazardly among their vegetables to give a bit of colour to their own gardens. From the early seventeenth century people laid out formal beds and borders, although fashions changed from neat herbal beds near the house, to

The golden-leaved yew, Taxus baccata *'Adpressa Variegata', and* Physocarpus opulifolius *'Dart's Gold' contrast with the pokers of kniphofia in the swirling patterns of a mixed informal border.*

great landscaped parklands, then back to intensively bedded and cosseted parterre borders, to the wilder styles of William Robinson (1838–1935). Then Gertrude Jekyll (1843–1932) brought her influence to bear, and the planting in 'rooms' around a house, with everything carefully colour schemed, was brought to its apogee. The style was refined and made more romantic at Hidcote and Sissinghurst, and now the sophisticated English cottage garden style is copied all over the world.

Today it is difficult to choose from the cornucopia of plants that is available and a plantsman's garden at the end of the twentieth century is too often a jumble, the beds and borders so crammed with rarities that they become like zoos full of strange inhabitants but with no style at all. Successful gardeners think of the overall effect and try to fit their impulse buys, those plants that they just must have, into an overall plan that is flexible enough to accommodate almost any eventuality. You may, for example, develop a sudden passion for the dahlia family and have to find homes for several in a stylish setting. Try them in pots on a terrace or patio, or introduce them into your beds so that the colours harmonize with the existing scheme. A pink and green bed or border with some white will allow you to add a pot of purple, shocking pink or even crimson dahlias in without any trouble. The clash and contrast of colours will add spice to the whole effect.

PLANNING BEDS AND BORDERS

When you plan the layout of the beds and borders, take a line from the house. Look out from each window and try to make a complete garden picture, designing the beds so that they focus on each one. Try a little formality near to the house – after all not many houses have portholes for windows, so circles and ovals are hard to tie in to the oblongs of traditional windows. As you move further away from the house, introduce curving borders, and if your garden merges into a rural landscape it is imperative to have some extra informality.

In a small garden walls, hedges and fences make excellent background for planting schemes and give a border a good skeleton on which to hang its designer clothes. If you have a wall, fence or hedge that faces the midday sun, always make your most important bed or border there. The plants will be protected from wind and will get all the sun that is going. Even the smallest garden can be divided into 'rooms' by the careful use of fences and hedges or sections of trellis, which will give height for colourful climbers to back beds and form little secret gardens to give an air of mystery to the tiniest backyard. Backgrounds are important in more formal gardens, too. Most period houses need the formality of straight lines and a considered design. A modern or post-1900 house can take the swirls and exuberance of island beds, but they have to be carefully planted to get height and depth without staking.

A formal border links the architecture of the house to the garden. Mounds of Berberis thunbergii *'Atropurpurea Nana' are repeated and echoed by the glorious colours of the stand of* Dahlia *'Bishop of Llandaff'.*

One of the easiest ways to lay out a new bed or border or to re-align an old one is to use a hosepipe. It can be laid in a straight line or in easy curves to give you an idea on the ground of just what your design will look like. It is even easier to go upstairs, if you have a house, to study the lines from an upstairs window so that you can see if you have skimped a curve or made a border too mean.

Always make your final decisions on the beds or borders that are close to the house from inside. Look through each window to see that you are making beautiful garden pictures, and aim to make things line up or curve dramatically but centrally. It is much more satisfactory to mass colour effects and beautiful forms where vistas and perspectives have been carefully considered.

If you have a small, modern garden you may have to forego traditional beds and borders, with their tiered plantings. If your planting areas are really only ribbons, try to avoid a 'spotty' effect by having just one of everything. It is far better to make one big statement with a strong architectural, preferably evergreen, plant and to choose just a few good plants set in large drifts.

Make access to the beds and borders easy. Wide areas definitely look better than narrow, but that can be difficult in a small garden. In large gardens both beds and borders are often up to 6m (20ft) wide, but they present their own difficulties, for the plants are hard to get at and work has to be done from a plank to avoid compacting the soil. It is often helpful to place stepping-stones strategically and as invisibly as possible, and if you can afford it, edge each border with stone so that nepetas (catmint) and pinks, which like to sprawl forwards, will not kill the lawn grasses. Do not cage beds that are set in lawns, however – it makes them look far too much like jam tarts.

Try to get as much depth as possible so that shrubs and groups of plants can be properly spaced to allow you to appreciate their shapes and flowers to the full. This is, of course, a counsel of perfection, and often perfection is boring – plants that drift together, climb into shrubs and flop over the edges are the most romantic plantings.

PLANTING FOR CLIMATE AND SOIL TYPE

Whatever shape or size you choose for your beds and borders, there are two factors that will determine how you plant them: the climate and the soil type.

If you live in a hot, dry place, your garden will be dominated by silver plants and those with succulent leaves – or it should be. But most of us long to grow exciting plants that offer a challenge to our skills, and we choose to add piles of heavy material, like manure, to our soil to improve its water retention so that we can grow those lovely large-leaved subjects that wilt at the first drought. Wherever you live you will find your gardening curtailed by the weather in some way, and you will learn to live with it.

The light, or lack of it, is often peculiar to your own garden. Large trees may dominate a large part of it or house walls may block the sun for most of the day, so that much of the garden is in perpetual shade. These are often the most exciting places to plant, for they offer ideal conditions for some of the most desirable hellebores, early bulbs and lilies.

The ecology of the garden will also help you to decide on the basic design of your beds and borders. If there are large trees, a pond or boggy area, dry, sandy conditions or hot, windy areas you will have to work around them.

In addition, you will have to take into account the soil type. It may be heavy clay, chalk, sand, moorland or even the extremes of desert or swamp. Nature clothes them all with suitable vegetation, and you will have to temper your ambitions to the requirements of your soil. Rhododendrons and heather flourish on peaty soils and sand, but they will not grow on chalky downlands or heavy clay, where roses and perennial plants will flourish. Wise gardeners follow nature's guiding hand and adapt their ideas to the garden rather than the other way around. Look around your neighbourhood to see what kind of plants grow well and make your plans accordingly. If you must have rhododendrons but have only chalk soil, buy a large container or two and fill with the right soil.

Natural Rhythms

In environmentally sound gardens – not just organically based gardens – the latest fashion is to take all natural factors into account. The Germans are leading the field in this sort of gardening, which aims to do away with all obvious artificiality. Their public gardens are being planted to follow the natural rhythms of the wild. Each bed and border is planted to give an almost continuous succession of flowers, and although they are still using perennial plants from all over the world, these are mingled throughout the beds, not grouped in broad drifts of a single variety as has been usual since the days of Gertrude Jekyll. Undulating carpets are formed, with shrubs and tall plants used to create excitement. Groups of the same perennial are planted throughout an area to look as if they have colonized naturally. The aim is to have good-looking, disease-free plant communities that are almost maintenance free. It is rather like an established wild-flower meadow in which the best-suited plants seed and thrive.

If plants are introduced that suit the ecology of the soil in your garden they should need little or no watering, feeding or staking. When plants choose to seed themselves they usually grow very happily, so if you can classify your garden as, say, woodland edge, marsh or rich ground, you choose the plants that will grow best there, improving the soil with suitable nutrients – grit, chalk or leaf-mould – but never with manure or nitrogenous fertilizers.

Gardeners who take care of large, famous gardens practise something similar because they have to have beds and borders that are colourful at all seasons. Oft-repeated clumps of plants, like nepetas (catmint) and lavender, create a dominant theme, which is followed by buddleias and aconites to give a similar, equally dominant effect with colour at a different season. But such gardeners do use more exotic species as well and feed them heavily.

Do not allow any of the really rampant growers to become established. Some of the more popular ground coverers, like vinca and the more prolific geraniums, must be banned. Instead, plants like asters, grasses, campanulas, bergenias, hemerocallis and asphodels, with their beautiful foliage, flowers and seedheads, should be chosen to flow right through each bed and border.

COLOUR BASICS

Colour is the most exciting aspect of gardening to tackle. Several hard and fast rules about how it should be used in planting schemes have been laid down by experts. There is also the classic colour wheel, which uses primary and secondary colours to demonstrate the shades that go together or that contrast with each other. Complementary colours – that is, those colours that are opposite each other in the spectrum such as red and green – go together, as do harmonizing colours – that is, those that are next to each other on the colour wheel and have similar tones such as red and blue. It is a very complicated subject, and whole books have been written on the subject.

The bright yellow of Tulipa '*Monte Carlo*' *and piercing blue of grape hyacinth,* Muscari armeniacum, *are perfect examples of the way colours from very opposite sides of the colour wheel can be combined.*

There are, in fact, very few colours that do not go together, and in the garden this is even more true than for houses because there is always the predominant green from foliage to leaven everything.

Some American gardeners have written that all reds go together, and that all pinks, all blues, all greens and all yellows go together. However, while mauves and blues can be striking, purples and blues can look funereal. On the other hand, bright, deep reds look wonderful with strong blues, although this is difficult to bring off successfully. Pink and yellow is an even more difficult combination, but someone like Christopher Lloyd, a guru of gardening on both sides of the Atlantic, happily breaks all the rules of colour theory and recommends such a colour scheme. In his hands it looks wonderful – in less talented hands it looks rather awful.

The more timid gardeners among us should stick to the rules, at least to begin with, and remember that all plants are moveable if we do make a terrible mistake. White always looks marvellous with any other colour and particularly on its own in an all-white scheme. Blues and yellows go together and look well – a golden-leaved shrub looks wonderful with a blue clematis wound into it.

Try to make all the things in your garden harmonize with each other, especially if it is a small garden with narrow borders and small beds. A bank of heather, a clump of silver birches and rhododendrons in soft pastel colours make a lovely picture, but do not try to brighten it up with a group of scarlet geraniums to give some summer colour. The flimsy subjects of colour scheming can be moved annually if necessary until you hit on the scheme that is exactly right for you.

Large Trees

Large trees are not usually part of a colour scheme, and they can be a problem in the traditional garden, although they would probably suit the new German way. However, if the plot is small, the tree dominant but a garden is wanted, there are solutions. Large trees are sometimes subject to protection orders, so you should check with the appropriate planning authority if you want to have it taken down. It is possible to learn to live with a large tree – you can have a mass of ivy underneath and very little else and just love the atmosphere – but the true gardener can do something with even the largest tree.

Stand and look at it. Decide whether you should have some of the lower branches removed, getting advice from a tree surgeon if you are at all uncertain. The canopy of a large, dominant beech, for example, could be thinned and lowered by an experienced arboriculturist. You could then grow many more plants in the beds below where before only early-flowering bulbs and the ubiquitous ivy could thrive.

Large evergreen trees can present more intractable problems. However, even a yew tree, with a dramatic evergreen canopy, can be retained and a bed made around it to bring it into a garden. It will require patience, much top-dressing of heavy manure and as much water as possible, but the ground around it can be transformed into a flowering border. A strong-growing species clematis, such as

C. potaninii var. *potaninii* (syn. *C. fargesii* var. *souliei*), could be planted to climb slowly up the rough trunk to throw its smoky grey flower garlands over the dark branches. Underneath a carpet of winter- and spring-flowering cyclamen, the cottage garden red valerian, *Centranthus ruber*, drifts of honesty, *Lunaria annua*, the sweet woodruff, *Gallium odoratum* (syn. *Asperula odorata*), with its starry, white, sweet-scented flowers would grow right up to the trunk. Plant *Iris foetidissima* var. *citrina*, which spreads into fan-shaped clumps, and *Rosa pimpinellifolia* 'Dunwich Rose', which used to colonize the dry Suffolk coastal dunes, to run into this planting. The tiny, fern-like foliage of the rose covers low-growing suckering stems, which will march right up to the yew, are covered for weeks with pale lemon flowers. At the edge of the yew canopy, *Rosa* 'Penelope' and *R.* 'Vanity' will reach up into the branches, which sweep low to the ground. To accompany them could be Canadian Preston hybrid lilac, *Syringa* × *josiflexa* 'Bellicent', with its pink spires in spring that then link into beds of other roses and herbaceous perennials.

The flowering plants under the tree – valerian, honesty and woodruff – are considered to be weeds by many plantsmen, but they are tough natives that will combine beautifully with the more precious plants that star in the border.

CORNERS AND EDGES

Corners and edges of beds are very important. Corners, for example, need a presence that will reflect the character of the bed. Yuccas, plain green or variegated in shades of cream or yellow, are dramatic and provide a full-stop to a corner. More traditional box, shaped into balls, is a classic addition and, in the variegated forms, can be colourful.

The woolly, silver-hued foliage of cotton lavender, *Santolina chamaecyparissus* (syn. *S. incana*), can be clipped into neat shapes, and it is excellent on a corner, surrounded by *Stachys byzantina* (syn. *S. lanata*, *S. olympica*). The stachys, which is known as bunnies' ears or lamb's tongue, has velvety, fat, whitened leaves, which make the pair into a complete garden picture.

Use edging plants to soften the harsh edges of beds and to define the edges of borders. Slow-growing and clump-forming or weaving and crawling plants are the best, and they can be planted either in a row for a formal edge or in random clusters to move back into the taller plants to provide a chain of continuity for the garden. In more formal gardens it is traditional to use plants that can be clipped and then contained, but some people prefer drifts or bands of edging plants to stray backwards to bring the planted area together. It also adds interest if you vary the height of the plants along the edge of the border or bed. One large plant brought forward, as if it has seeded itself there naturally, brings an air of prodigality into the garden.

Traditional Lavender

Lavender has long been a favourite edging plant. It is one of the most aromatic shrubs and looks especially good if a border near a terrace is edged with stone. It is also perfect for rose beds and for edging grey or blue borders. Use *Lavandula*

The soft pink of Dianthus *'Lilian' and the purple of* Lavandula stoechas *ssp.* pendunculata *form a pretty edging for a border in a hot, dry garden.*

angustifolia 'Hidcote' for its narrow grey-green leaves and stems, its compact growth and dark violet spikes of flower. Try *L. angustifolia* 'Lodden Pink', 'Alba' (for white flowers) or the species, which used to be known as *L.* 'Vera', for a paler blue haze. The white lavender goes particularly well with the lax, pink, daisy-flowered *Osteospermum jucundum*, which is a hardy form of the tender pot plant. Only use this combination in a sheltered spot, but it looks beautiful in front of pink and purple roses, acanthus and *Salvia* × *sylvestris* 'May Night', with its dense flowers in deep purple.

Although box and clipped santolina look marvellous in a formal scheme, most edges benefit from the softening effect of encroaching plants. Lady's mantle, *Alchemilla mollis*, is a plant that can do little wrong – except seed itself rather prolifically. Its deeply scalloped leaves and arching sprays of lime green flowers make it an excellent edger for both modern or cottage garden styles. It goes with most herbaceous perennials, but looks especially good with groups of *Euphorbia characias* ssp. *wulfenii* and bergenias, and it always looks lovely when combined with old fashioned roses.

Bergenia in all its forms is one of the best edgers. It has huge leaves – the plant is nicknamed elephant's ears – which are shiny and deeply furrowed and which make the perfect contrast to grass, paving or gravel. They are evergreen, often turning vivid colours in winter. The flowers range in a colour from white through pink to deepest red. *Bergenia* 'Bressingham White' has dwarf leaves, so it is particularly good in a small garden, and *B.* 'Wintermärchen', a fairly new cultivar, has some of the best deep red leaves in winter.

Ideal edging plants are grasses which form stiff clumps. *Carex oshimensis* 'Evergold', striped in gold and green, makes miniature fountains of hard foliage, and *Festuca glauca*, blue fescue, makes little, steely blue, upright brushes. Plant these two edging plants in groups together and add taller *Berberis thunbergii* 'Atropurpurea Nana', with its purple foliage and neat, tiny leaves, to give a change of light at the front of a shady border where ferns, bergenias and geraniums would luxuriate.

Symphony in Pink

Alpines and small herbaceous perennials can be used to lower the height of a bed or border and to make a pretty, floriferous edging. *Phuopsis stylosa*, with its thread-like foliage and tiny corymbs of pink flowers, will weave into the fat, velvety leaves of *Geranium renardii*, Campanula portenschlagiana, with its tiny purple thimble flowers, is beautiful with *Geranium sanguineum* var. *striatum*, a tiny weaver with flat pink flowers. This symphony in pink and purple is stunning in front of silver artemisias such as *A.* 'Powis Castle'.

Mixing flowers and herbs is an old cottage garden habit, and it is an easy one to copy when it comes to edging. Many herbs are neat, tidy plants, and growing them close to paths makes it easy to pick them.

Origanum vulgare 'Aureum', the golden marjoram, is a brilliant edging or corner plant. It naturally makes a round dome of bright yellow leaves, which are enhanced by tiny mauve flowers in late summer. It is aromatic and actually likes partial shade.

Parsley, in its curled English form, *Petroselinum crispum*, makes a good crimped edging. Pour boiling water over the seeds to get them to germinate. It contrasts sweetly with chives, *Allium schoenoprasum*, which make neat clumps of edible, grassy leaves and flowers with pink or purple globe-shaped flowers, which are lovely in salads. Divide in spring to make more and more.

Thymes in their prostrate forms can be used to edge herb gardens, but their little bushy variants are better in herbaceous borders. Plant groups of *Thymus vulgaris* 'Silver Posie', which has white-edged leaves and pink flowers, next to drifts of the yellow-edged *Thymus citriodorus* 'Aureus', with its lemon-scented leaves for a silver and gold effect.

Edgings can help to tie a garden together, but plan for the huge mass of plants behind them by relying on foliage and form rather than on a mass of flower and plan to have some spectacular variegated or very large plants to create an interesting theatrical effect.

REPETITIVE OR MIRROR PLANTING

When you want to tie a planting of disparate elements together in a bed or border, repetitive or mirror planting is very useful. In Britain The National Trust makes use of this technique in some of its gardens, and it is effective in long borders, even though they could be just as beautiful in a smaller way and certainly make a good and easy picture. At Buscot Park at Farringdon, Oxfordshire, for example, groups of colourful trees, shrubs and perennials are planted regularly and repeatedly down each side of a long border.

The technique works beautifully for a one-sided border as well. The yellow-leaved *Robinia pseudoacacia* 'Frisia' dominates, as several specimens march at intervals down the border, underplanted with the pale gold foliage of *Philadelphus coronarius* 'Aureus', which, in turn, are interspersed with the purple foliage of different berberis.

Further forwards in the border are groups of *Phlomis fruticosa*, with its subtle furry khaki foliage, the bright silver leaves and golden flowers of *Brachyglottis* Dunedin hybrid 'Sunshine' (syn. *Senecio* 'Sunshine') and the lime green flower heads and glaucous blue-grey leaves of *Euphorbia characias* ssp. *wulfenii*. Yellow-flowered potentillas and the tiny-leaved *Lonicera nitida* 'Baggesen's Gold', a shrub that throws out branches almost like fern fronds, contrast with *Nepeta* 'Six Hill Giant' and its tremendous blue flowers, which grows towards the front of the border. *Alchemilla mollis*, the old-fashioned lady's mantle, with its sharp lime green flowers, *Lysimachia punctata*, towering up with its spires of yellow, and the silver soft ears of *Stachys byzantina* provide a perfect edge to the border. At Buscot there is a final touch – a neat box edging to give a formal look.

This sort of repetitive planting looks good when the gardener does not want to collect plants but prefers to try a selection. For instance, red-leaved berberis come in many different varieties, potentillas are available with a range of shades of flower and foliage, and there are many sorts of nepeta to try. All the herbaceous perennials could be changed from time to time as long as the colour scheme was followed. As the trees and shrubs grew and the ground-cover plants became established, there would be little weeding but a very stylish effect would be achieved.

There are so many different styles and fashions to choose among, and in many ways gardening is even more of a personal statement than wearing fashionable clothes. Two gardeners may grow the same plants but each will make his or her own statement – hardly any gardens are the same unless they were designed and planted by one person.

STARS IN THE BORDER

Plants are, of course, the essence of gardening. They are what gardeners are really excited about. But if the context is not right, it is impossible to convey that excitement to other gardeners, who, on the whole, like nothing better than doing a leaf-by-leaf inspection of their own or someone else's garden.

Cottage gardens have always contained a mixture of plants in the flower borders, including quite a lot of vegetables, but in larger gardens segregation was practised as long as there was paid labour to do most of the work. Even today it is sometimes possible to find one of these traditional but time-, labour- and space-extravagant gardens. At one time, for example, irises were grown in strictly segregated gardens, and although there is no better way to show off a collection of the old bearded irises and today's smaller medium plants, that part of the garden inevitably looks tatty and unexciting for ten months of the year.

Herbaceous borders, rose borders, shrubberies and bedded-out annuals used all to be kept rigorously secluded, but nowadays we do not find that kind of strict regime attractive, and the mixed border has become the accepted way of making the garden beautiful for every month of the year. A modern exception to this is the hosta and grass bed, which is a fashionable green foliage alternative to flowers. This move began in the United States, where grasses have been used with tremendous success in the James Van Sweden gardens and are now finding a following in Europe. A small corner of a tiny garden devoted to these two plants makes an emerald oasis in a sea of colour, and they mix well with the shrubs that give solidity, form and some flower.

Shrubs also often provide the foliage texture that makes the perfect background for the great drifts of colour provided by herbaceous perennials, the dashing and exciting elements of a border. On their own, they can look like so much coloured hay, but carefully juxtaposed for foliage effect, flower colour and shape, they are thrilling. Set off by great magnolias and, later, lilies they make for true inspiration. Indeed, lilies, along with all the other spring and summer bulbs, can be worked into all these plantings.

Many gardeners no longer bother with bedding plants for beds and borders, preferring to use them in tubs and containers where they provide instant, easy colour. Nevertheless, intriguing effects can be achieved by the judicious use of annuals, such as nicotianas, lavateras and poppies, which give a garden a lift later in the year when the first fine flush of summer is over. If they are allowed to self-sow, wild flowers such as cornflowers, corncockles, poppies and verbascums, and annuals, such as love-in-a-mist, *Nigella damascena*, can colonize difficult parts of the garden and colour them in great misty swathes throughout the summer.

To keep beds and borders interesting at all times, use Gertrude Jekyll's trick of dropping in the odd pot of something exotic. Take a green and white striped agave in a terracotta or oriental-style container and place it carefully against a small-leaved, early-flowering shrub that is a dead spot in the border and you have a new talking point. The agave needs sun, so do not let it become embowered with foliage, but it needs little water, so it will forgive you if you forget to water it once or twice.

Cottage garden plants mingle happily, creating swirls of colour. Hypericum *'Hidcote' dominates large clumps of* Stachys byzantina *'Silver Carpet', blue eryngiums and* Sedum aïzoön.

PLANTING FOR SUCCESSION

It takes thought and care to achieve a bed or border that looks ravishing throughout the year. In midsummer it is easy to have shrub or modern roses in bloom and honeysuckle perfuming the air. Irises – a rainbow of bearded and Siberian blues and purples, reds and yellows – sumptuous maroon and pink peonies and oriental poppies in pinks and scarlets rampage through the garden. At this time of the year, too, the hardy geraniums in their myriad shades sprawl along the edges, with *Alchemilla mollis*, lady's mantle, interjecting its sharp note of lime. In summer tufts of pinks, *Dianthus* ssp., in all their many forms of spiky grey foliage and clove-scented flowers, mingle with all the flowers to fill our beds and borders with colour and perfume. But when they have gone, what happens in the winter, the spring and the autumn? What advance planning strategies can we adopt to make sure that our gardens are filled with colour and shape throughout the rest of the year?

Layered Look

If you have mixed borders and beds you can have the layered look. Evergreens will form a background against which the summer stars will shine. Spring bulbs will spear through the dormant perennial plants to make a flowery mead and later their untidy dying foliage will be hidden by the burgeoning delicate leaves of day lilies and geraniums. Roses and shrubs – deutzias, with their delicate corymbs of pink or white flowers, or philadelphus, with sweetly scented scads of blossom – take up the story in early summer and later can be hung with the gorgeous flowers of a clematis. After the glorious flush of summer come the quieter flowers of the hydrangeas, ranging from the lavender shades of *Hydrangea aspera* Villosa Group (syn. *H. villosa*) to the deep purple-red of *H.* 'Preziosa', which tone with the soft colours of asters and Michaelmas daisies.

As well as the early bulbs, summer bulbs can be planted into the herbaceous sections with roses. Include galtonias, *Galtonia candicans* and *G. viridiflora*, with their steepled white and green bells from midsummer onwards, the magnificent *Allium* family and the huge, exciting tribe of lilies, which go perfectly with shrubs, perennials and even grasses and hostas.

As autumn sets in, the pink and white Japanese anemones, *Anemone* × *hybrida*, tone with the blue of agapanthus, the soft mauves and crimsons of fuchsias, and the flat, dusty pinks of *Sedum spectabile*. By the time autumn has really set in, the mixed beds and borders are still dominated by the blues of the wolfsbane, *Aconitum carmichaelii*, and the unusual liriope, *Liriope muscari*, with its spikes of bright blue flowers.

Borders without flowers

It is possible to go for the easy option and plant only shrubs in your beds and borders. This is supposed to be labour saving, and indeed bulbs have to be planted or re-planted every year and herbaceous perennials have to be divided regularly to keep them flowering at their best and, worst of all, have to be cut down each year to keep a border looking tidy, all of which is hard work.

Shrubberies, as the Victorians called them, have got a bad name recently because they can look so dull for much of the year, but this need not be the case. It is possible to have a beautiful border of shrubs by using coloured foliage and many evergreens.

An artful use of shrubs would include planting groups of berberis in all their many foliage and berry colours. They do flower, albeit unobtrusively, and fruit colourfully, but it is for their coloured leaves that most are grown. The red-purple of *Berberis thunbergii* 'Rose Glow' with the pale blue of the spruce *Picea pungens* var. *glauca* makes a strange and beautiful combination. Add a *Pinus mugo* in the background for its strong, bright green whorls and a *Juniperus* × *media* 'Pfitzeriana' to add a feathery touch at the front of the border. A silvery *Pyrus salicifolia* 'Pendula', with its long streams of silver leaves could be surrounded with clipped balls of a berberis such as *B. thunbergii* 'Atropurpurea Nana'.

Combinations of this sort are permanent once planted and need as little maintenance as it is possible to have in a garden and still give a dramatic effect. In fact, your garden will be as colourful at all seasons as your flower beds are in summer. There is only one problem – it is always the same colourful self, lacking the sparkle and dynamism of a flower bed or border. By all means adopt this style if you have little time, and use it as a background for masses of tiny spring bulbs, which will bring life and flowers and which can be left to naturalize.

Shape and Texture

A planting scheme that does not rely on coloured foliage as much as on good shapes and textures would have to include *Genista aetnensis*, the Mount Etna broom, which is perfect to give height in a shrub border or an island bed of shrubs. It grows into a tall fountain of green, thread-like branches, which are veiled in golden flowers in midsummer. Its greatest asset is that, although tree-like, it is almost leafless and practically anything will grow below it.

Combine the broom with *Rubus cockburnianus* in its latest form, Golden Vale, which has the palest primrose, vine-shaped leaves and pale silvery stems all winter. The stems must be cut down to the ground at the end of winter to produce a new flush of the whitewashed stems and entrancing leaves. For bulk at the front of this grouping add two or three mahonias – *M.* × *media* 'Winter Sun' or 'Buckland' have handsome foliage and bright yellow flowers in late autumn. They, too, can be heavily trimmed in March to keep them in order.

At the very front of the border add *Choisya ternata* 'Sundance', with its shining yellow leaves and sparkling white flowers in late spring and sometimes in late summer as well. The foliage is a real winner, and when it is picked for flower arrangements has the bonus of a strange, strong scent. Cheating slightly, but it is a climbing shrub, add a clematis like the latest and most fashionable Japanese 'Edomurasaki', which has dark violet petals with white stamens. To reinforce this blue theme, add a *Buddleia davidii* 'Dartmoor' at the back of the border or in the centre of a bed. This is a graceful form, which has none of the coarseness of many of the *davidii* cultivars. It is multi-headed, with plumes of purple blossom from midsummer onwards.

Other good shrubs to add into this particular grouping would include a yucca at the front or corner of the border. This would anchor the airy presence of the other shrubs, and its own towering steeples of white flowers, which appear on mature plants, would be spectacular. Another good front-of-border evergreen is Jerusalem sage, *Phlomis fruticosa*, which has woolly grey foliage that looks as if it has been dipped in mustard powder and whorls of yellow flowers in summer.

Add a good *Hebe salicifolia*, a hardy plant with long, tapering, elegant evergreen leaves and sheaves of white, scented blossom in summer, and bulk up this grouping with one of the best of all shrubs, *Cornus alba* 'Elegantissima'. This has carmine red stems, which are overlaid all summer with the cleanest and freshest of white and green leaves.

If you have any more space, try to acquire a *Heptacodium miconioides*, which is becoming more common in cultivation. This member of the jasmine family, comes from China, and it has been propogated by the Arnold Arboretum in the United States. It grows into a pyramid of beauty, but it needs to form its own triangle within a shrub border or bed so that the amazing grace of its growth can be seen alone and its lovely white panicles of flowers, startling against a green background, can be appreciated to the full.

Phormiums, bamboos, like *Arundinaria viridistriata* with its rich yellow leaves, *Ruta graveolens* 'Jackman's Blue', the bitter rue of the Bible with its glaucous, cut leaves, box, rosemary, purple sage and lavenders with their purple, mauve, blue, pink and white flowers are all excellent, shapely plants for shrub borders.

Shrub borders and beds are the easiest to design, for it is easy to see the shape of each shrub, to know whether it is spiky, rounded, fountain-like or feathery and to place each in its best contrasting or complementary position. Flower colour matters not at all, although all the named plants have yellow, blue or white flowers, which make an exciting colour scheme of their own.

Trees to Try

One of the most tempting layers to attempt is to introduce trees, which will give height and depth to your mixed planting. Even a very small garden can accommodate one flowering tree that is strategically placed in a mixed group to give a different emphasis.

Overcome the temptation of buying a Japanese cherry, *Prunus* ssp., when you visit garden centres. These plants are so balletically beautiful in their pink frills in spring, but these blossoms are borne for only ten days or so, and afterwards they stand hugely plain in their beds for the rest of the year. They also sucker badly if their roots are disturbed, and because the roots run near the surface all over a flower bed they can create serious problems. If you cannot resist a tree like the Japanese cherry – the *Prunus* ssp. from other countries do not seem to sucker – choose a member of the *Malus* family, its close relation. *Malus floribunda*, for example, is a relatively small grower – it will reach 4.6m (15ft) and perhaps 2.4m (8ft) wide in fifteen years – and it can be pruned and trimmed carefully to a good shape so that even out of flower it looks presentable. In flower it is a marvel of delicacy, with a cloud of tiny red buds that open to showers of palest pink in late

The pinks and red of phlox and the yellow achillea combine to create a wonderful contrast with clumps of sedum and spires of Macleaya cordata.

spring. Grow a *Clematis viticella* 'Purpurea Plena Elegans' into it for a later flowering of double violet pompons that last from midsummer until early autumn. The clematis must be cut hard back in early spring so that the tree is left to flower unencumbered by old stems.

Malus 'Golden Hornet', a crab apple, is also a good tree for a flower bed or border. It has drifts of white apple blossom in late spring, followed by a treasure trove of golden fruits, which appear in early autumn and last throughout winter. It does not appear to sucker at all, roses and shrubs will grow into its shade, and it seems to be the perfect tree for even a fairly small garden.

An exception to the Japanese cherry rule must be *Prunus × subhirtella* 'Autumnalis', which is the most fragile creature imaginable but which unbelievably bursts into showers of tiny flowers in late autumn. In good years, it flowers right through until the end of spring. Its fine tracery of black branches dance with blossom through the worst winds and frost, and it is only set back by really ferocious weather. Even after the worst winters it will set to and flower its heart out for many weeks. It can be carefully pruned into shape, cut right back to keep it from outgrowing its space in a border, and it will take a clematis, such as 'Perle d'Azur' with its china blue flowers all summer, into its bosom. This clematis can be partly pruned in late autumn before the *Prunus* flowers. Take out all the old clambering growths that are obscuring the branches and finish by pruning hard back in early spring.

Koelreutaria paniculata, sometimes known as the golden rain tree or the pride of India, is another great candidate for a mixed border. It is not reliably hardy, but in a sheltered garden it achieves an interesting bonsaied outline by the time it is fifteen years old. The ferny pink-tinted leaves open early, so they can be damaged by frost, but they always repeat the trick and come again. Late in the summer yellow panicles of foxglove-like flowers appear all over the tree just when you need colour, and in winter the flowers convert into large bladder pods of seed, which dry exceedingly well for flower arrangements. It is truly a tree for all seasons.

If you grow something like a *Clematis montana* var. *sericea* (syn. *C. chrysocoma* var. *sericea*) into it you get several delights. The clematis is more elegant than many of the *montana* persuasion, and it has serrated leaves, silver flowers, and a strong sweet smell in late spring. It must be pruned judiciously – not at all if possible, but cut it back after flowering if you have to. The koelreutaria can take quite a lot of it in its stride, but cut out large stems every two or three years if you are worried that the clematis is becoming overwhelming.

Catalpa bignonioides, the Indian bean tree, is another good candidate for the flower border. It is medium sized with giant leaves. It grows fast and has rather a coarse trunk and wide-spreading branches. It comes into leaf late in the spring and then the soft furry greenness is enticing on its own. Because it is so late leafing, many climbers make use of its wide crown to make their homes. Try *Clematis* 'Guernsey Cream', which has enormous, subtle creamy-green flowers that decorate the catalpa's branches before the leaves appear. Add one of the rampant ground-covering roses – 'Swany', for example, which will just lift into the lower branches for a second flowering in early summer – and then wait for the catalpa to do its stuff. In midsummer (earlier in sheltered spots) it sends up huge foxglove-like buds at the tips of each shoot, and the white flowers with their yellow and purple markings are borne in conspicuous panicles. The tree never seems to get so tall that you cannot get among its branches and look right into the flowers. There is the added bonus of long strings of magnificent beans. Many garden centres now stock the yellow-leaved catalpa, and the foliage is lovely, but the flowers, if they appear, look unattractive against the yellow leaves. There is a wonderful newer, purple-leaved and purple-stemmed version that would look magnificent in similar border situations, but it is difficult to find.

One of the only trees planted in the rose garden at Sissinghurst, which is now more of a mixed border garden, is a version of the bird cherry, *Prunus padus* 'Colorata'. Its dark purplish shoots, copper-purple young foliage and pale pink flowers are a stylish combination that fits elegantly into a border. Its trunk is slender and its head light, and if the gardeners of Sissinghurst consider it suitable for bedding work it must be a good subject that does not sucker.

Robinia pseudoacacia 'Frisia' is a tall, thin tree with truly golden leaves, and it is often used in large gardens to give height and colour in a flower bed or border. It has rather brittle branches, and if these are damaged and brought down in high winds they may cause havoc in a densely planted bed. *Gleditsia triacanthos* 'Sunburst' is a good alternative if you want a very bright accent in a bed.

CHAPTER 2

BURSTING OF SPRING

SPRING IS SUPPOSED TO begin at the vernal equinox, that day on which day and night are of equal length, but scientists tell us that the growing season really starts when the soil temperature at a depth of 30cm (12in) is above 6°C (43°F). Only then, when the soil reaches this optimum temperature will roots start to develop on grass, evergreens, many bulbs and early herbaceous plants.

Many people long for spring gardens that bulge with flowering azaleas and rhododendrons, camellias and magnolias. However, these plants require acid soil and a high rainfall, and most of us have to struggle to grow them successfully. Instead, we rely on the equally pretty but less demanding shrubs of springtime. In fact, gardens that rely too heavily on the rhododendron family are sometimes heavy with gloomy foliage by midsummer, whereas in gardens where spring bulbs are grouped with good foliage plants there is space for later summer stars and the evergreen background will be of the whole range of shades.

The film of green that comes over the bare soil and the trees and the first flowers that thrust through the earth mean that the gardening year has truly begun. Primroses and violets are among the first to appear, although some will have started to bloom in what is, technically, winter if the weather has been mild. The sweet violet, *Viola* ssp. will carpet the ground under shrubs and the back of borders. There is nothing quite like a sea of violets in their shades of purple, blue, pink and white to give a taste of the bounty to come, while pale yellow primroses, *Primula* ssp. shine out from evergreen thickets and seed happily.

Borders and beds seem wider and flatter at this time of the year, and they need a festival of flowers before the main show starts. Bulbs are the first cultivated arrivals, and they raise the curtain for the great scene-stealers of spring, the flowering trees and shrubs. Bulbs give another dimension to the bare earth and carpet it with bright colour when everything else is brown and green. Most people prefer pale, subtle colours and choose to shadow their beds with drifts of blue chionodoxas and scillas, to raise the eye with clouds of moonlight soft narcissus and to delve into the shade of shrubs with sweeps of windflowers, *Anemone blanda*.

If you like bright primary colours, this is the time of the year when an artistic eye can get away with it in a garden context. Consider Sissinghurst and the spring walk, where Sir Harold Nicolson brought off a triumph in vulgar colours. There are the brightest scarlets, vivid blues, startling yellows and every colour combination in stripes and bi-colours that can be imagined. But it is brilliant because it is carefully controlled and because it is hedged and embowered in green. This kind of garden can be successful only where it is in a hidden part of a bed, where it is glimpsed suddenly and unexpectedly and where it does not jar with, say, a serene white border.

CROCUSES FOR EARLY COLOUR

Crocuses, especially the species, appear when it is still winter, while others delight us in early spring. Sadly, driving winds and rain often ruin the tiniest almost as soon as the flowers open.

A few *Crocus tommasinianus* tucked into a border will bring the thrill of a sheet of silvery blue on the first sunny day. They quickly naturalize and within a few years will have turned into a carpet. Plant them at the edge of borders or, if you can afford to, in great drifts sweeping through the beds. The variety *C. tommasinianus* 'Whitewell Purple' has slender, rich violet-purple flowers with bright marigold yellow stamens. Even when they are battered by the weather, they lie like a taffeta shawl on the soil to provide a hint of spring.

Crocus chrysanthus, another early crocus, is lovely in the border, and there are many colours – 'Blue Pearl', 'Cream Beauty', 'Snow Bunting' and the purple 'Ladykiller', to name only a few. Later flowering crocuses include *C. vernus* 'Pickwick', which is white heavily feathered with purple and which stands up to a good deal of bad weather. The flowers are larger than in the species, and 'Pickwick' has several cousins – 'Queen of the Blues', 'Yellow Mammoth' and 'Striped Beauty' – which all live up to their names. Unlike narcissi, crocuses have the added beauty of delicate, even pretty, leaves that disappear without trace under the rising tide of spring foliage.

Crocuses are the easiest small bulbs to tuck into a planting scheme. They can surround and be planted into groups of plants like agapanthus and *Alchemilla mollis* and will burst through the foliage of helianthemums and even decorate the stumps of *Artemisia* 'Powis Castle', which needs a trim as the crocuses develop. Under a *Malus* 'Golden Hornet' (see Fig. 1) a sea of crocus will echo the white blossom overhead. The ceanothus and perovskia are added to the planting scheme to take it through to autumn, when their blue flowers will contrast with the yellow fruits on the *Malus*. *Euphorbia myrsinites*, with its yellow spring flowers, will be a foil for the fragile crocuses, and the holly will intensify the gold effect.

DANCING DAFFODILS

Spring would not be spring without daffodils dancing in our gardens, but they can be difficult to place in beds and borders. Their thick, juicy leaves need many weeks to take up enough food to nurture the bulb for another year, and they must be left *in situ*, as they gradually age and yellow, spoiling many a well-designed scheme. Although the flowers are beautiful, therefore, only the small narcissi should be considered for the small garden. Plant the larger ones in pots,

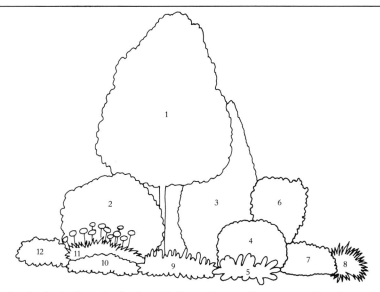

Fig. 1 *A spring border for underplanting with blue, white or yellow crocuses, chionodoxas or scillas.*

1 *Malus* 'Golden Hornet'
2 *Ceanothus* × *delileanus* 'Gloire de Versailles'
3 *Ilex* × *altaclerensis* 'Golden King'
4 *Artemisia* 'Powis Castle'
5 *Euphorbia myrsinites*
6 *Perovskia* 'Blue Spire'
7 *Alchemilla mollis*
8 *Holcus mollis* 'Albovariegatus'
9 *Liriope muscari*
10 *Helianthemum* 'Wisley Primrose'
11 *Agapanthus campanulatus*
12 *Ajuga reptans* 'Rainbow'

so that you can enjoy them in groups in the garden, either sunk into beds so that they can be replaced with bedding plants later in the season, or as lovely container plants. If your garden is small and you cannot tuck them under shrubs at the back of the border, give them away after they have flowered.

No garden is too small for a few of the smaller narcissi, and some of the best of the miniatures are *N.* 'Jack Snipe', a traditional but small, perfect daffodil; 'Jenny', a graceful white; 'Peeping Tom', the earliest, which lasts for weeks; 'Minnow', with pale petals and deeper cup; 'Tête-à-Tête', the best miniature; 'April Tears', with many heads to each stem; and 'Rippling Waters', with delicate heads of three ice white flowers with reflexed petals.

For late spring there are four unusual narcissi that mix well with other early spring flowers. *N.* 'Thalia', which is known as the orchid-flowered narcissus, is the essence of spring. The flowers seem to be carried in a hand-tied posy – each stem has several pure white flowers with fluted petals. Teamed with a *Viburnum* × *burkwoodii*, its delicate flowers will shine against the dark evergreen of the shrub and contrast with it fragrant umbels of white flowers. Planted under *Magnolia* × *loebneri* 'Leonard Messel', which is one of the easiest of the lime-tolerant, spring-flowering magnolias with its wispy pink and white flowers, it is a true essay in springtime.

N. 'Hawera' is a delight. It is a small cultivar, about 20cm (8in) high, with many nodding heads of flowers, like minute dancing yellow stars. 'Rip van

Drifts of Anemone blanda *'White Splendour' are pierced with groups of the dainty* Narcissus *known as 'Jack Snipe'.*

Winkle' is a curious little plant, which was discovered in Ireland. It is almost like a dandelion, with its shaggy petals and round face, but it is delicately beautiful and looks wonderful with scads of muscari at the front of a border. 'Sun Disc' is another strange narcissus. It has a completely flat face, just like a disc, that faces up to the sun and reflects its shine. All these smaller narcissi fit neatly into flower beds to give a dazzling display very early and highlight the colours of spring-flowering shrubs.

BULBS TO PLANT IN DRIFTS

Anemone blanda, the windflowers of spring, are the freshest of flowers to drift through a border, and once planted they are there for ever. First, the ferny leaves with a purple tinge break through the bare earth, then dozens of flowers appear in shades of blue, pink and a dazzling white *A. blanda* 'White Splendour'. *A. blanda* 'Blue Mist' is one of the most versatile, for it makes a carpet of blossom around shrubs and is most effective among old fashioned roses, where it will weave into their bare stems after a few years. They are horrid to plant for they arrive in little packets as tiny brittle tubers, which appear to be nothing worth having. Scrape away some soil and lay them in your planned groups and then recover them. Some people recommend soaking overnight before planting.

Chionodoxas and scillas in their blue form are most beautiful planted around groups of narcissi. Chionodoxa, commonly known as the glory of the snow, often flowers earlier, but some years the two coincide. *C. Forbesii* is a form of the old variety known as 'Cambridge Blue'; it has a large white centre and is loved by early butterflies, *C. Luciliae* has large flowers of gentian blue with a lavender flush and an almost ice white centre, *C. sardensis* has deep blue buds opening to royal blue flowers which make an intense patch of colour. There is also a pink variety, *C. Forbesii* 'Pink Giant', which is a larger plant. It has strong, upright stems and extremely beautiful flowers, which are unusual at this time of the year. They are rose pink and are the perfect accompaniment for early cherry blossom.

Scillas are equally good for naturalizing, and they make pools of strong blue to contrast with the yellow buds of dwarf narcissi. The most commonly seen is *S. siberica*, a beauty with cobalt blue petals that shade into royal blue. *S. siberica* 'Spring Beauty' has bright china blue flowers with a touch of ultramarine; it is larger than the species and flowers for much longer. Drifted together they make a fantastic sight under deciduous trees.

WOODLAND BEAUTIES

For a cool border in the shade of a tree, where hydrangeas and dicentras are waiting to give colour later, there is nothing more elegant than the erythronium, the dog's tooth violet. The hybrid *Erythronium* 'Pagoda' has wonderfully marbled foliage, which spreads over the bare soil, providing its own ground cover for the tall stems of canary yellow flowers suspended like the roofs of pagodas. The petals are reflexed like a lily to show off the cinnamon coloured anthers, which give a graceful air to the lovely sprays. This native of California grows in the woodlands of the foothills of the Sierra Nevada, but it settles down to increase happily in well-drained soil enriched with leaf mould.

Many other erythroniums naturalize in cultivated beds in partial shade. *E. Californicum* 'White Beauty; is one of the best because it increases fast in leafy soil under trees – perfect for those with difficult shady borders.

THE FRATERNITY OF FRITILLARIES

Fritillaries are subtle and quietly decorative spring flowers. A native British species, *Fritillaria meleagris*, is slowly disappearing in the wild, but it has become quite fashionable as an easy self-seeding member of the best flowerbeds. Its dangling, bell-shaped flowers are either intriguingly chequered and shaded with purple over white or are pure, pristine white. They flower for weeks and are sophisticated companions for primroses, epimediums and pale lemon and white wallflowers.

More spectacular is *F. imperialis*, the proud crown imperial, with its drooping orange or yellow bells ruffed with gleaming green. This is a tall plant, over 1m (3ft) high in the right conditions, and it has a strange, foxy smell. It likes a sunny, open position and it looks best spearing up through a carpet of herbaceous perennials that will take the stage later on. To keep it flowering year after year, give it a dressing of sulphate of potash in spring and autumn.

Damp shade under deciduous trees and shrubs will be colonized by Erythronium dens-canis *'White Splendour' and* Fritillaria meleagris.

All fritillaries are attractive or interesting, but some are more interesting than garden-worthy, and some are so difficult that they are only for a special greenhouse. In addition, ordinary gardeners will find it almost impossible to obtain them unless they are prepared to seek out specialist growers. Several can be grown from seed, however, and because they make unusual talking points for the spring border they are worth effort. *F. pontica*, *F. pallidiflora*, *F. pyrenaica* and *F. verticillata* are particularly interesting. They like a moist, leafy soil where they will show off their unusual creamy, greeny colours, and look especially charming with ferns in the shade of a lightly canopied tree. The fritillaries are among the flowers that gardeners grow to love after they have been through the colourful phase that we all enjoy at the beginning of our gardening careers.

BLUE WEEDS

The muscari, grape hyacinth, is a bulb that anyone can grow but will probably live to regret. The flowers are the most heavenly blue you have ever seen, but it has disastrous leaves, which are prolific before the flowers appear and a tangled mess afterwards. The seeds spread everywhere and take over the tiny treasures at the front of borders. The answer is to grow *M. armeniacum* 'Heavenly Blue' in pots, so that you can appreciate the full beauty of the flowers without the threat of their constant presence. They will multiply quickly, even in pots, and then they can be divided up, repotted and given as presents to all your friends.

In spring the stately orange Fritillaria imperialis *provides a striking contrast with the graceful white-flowered* Fritillaria verticillata.

In your beds and borders you can get the same blue effect in late spring with *M. latifolium*, which has lovely flowers, light blue top at the top of the spike and a rich purple-violet lower down. They do not increase, and in fact they can sometimes be difficult to keep going. *M. comosum* 'Plumosum', the feather hyacinth, has tassels of pale violet in late spring. The plants can be quite difficult to establish and they often die out if they are not happy in their particular setting. But they are certainly worth the effort.

Muscari is sometimes known as the 'heavenly blue weed', and although it is one of those plants that are difficult to do without, they must be eradicated from delicate plants and allowed to establish themselves only under the toughest shrubs and strong roses.

Exceptionally beautiful, but delicate, is the white form, *M. azureum* 'Album'. It is a must for white borders where it could be grouped or even make an edging where its tiny fragile flowers would hold their own against the still-dormant silvers of artemisia and oriental poppy.

Tiny lemon narcissi star a carpet of Muscari botryoïdes *and are surrounded by a drift of the bronze-foliaged* Libertia peregrinans.

TULIPOMANIA

Tulips are one of the plants that you may grow to like as you get older. Many young gardeners think they are too much trouble and even that they are stiff and too stately. Eventually, however, almost everybody finds them indispensable and wants more and more of them. In fact, it is almost impossible to imagine a spring garden without them.

Probably one of the problems with tulips is that the counsel of perfection says they should be lifted after flowering and once the foliage has died down. This is a great deal of trouble and means that somewhere safe has to be found to store them all summer long. Then they have to be re-planted in the autumn. Many people, however, prefer to plant them as deeply as possible – more than 20cm (8in) down – and leave them to get on with their lives. Some will multiply, others will not, but most will go on from year to year. The lily-flowered types and the doubles seem to do best in these conditions.

Bulb suppliers have recently introduced a plastic basket that will hold about ten bulbs. The basket is filled with compost and bulbs, then put in the ground where the tulips are to flower. As the leaves start to turn nasty, and they do, the basket is simply lifted so that the bulbs can dry off. They are then stored for replanting later. It is certainly easier than forking around for bulbs in a bed.

Late spring brings in the species tulips. Some naturalize easily in some gardens, others disappear after two or three seasons. Although they could be lifted, dried and replanted, they are cheap to buy – ten will cost the same as a bunch of florist's flowers and last years longer – and they may seed or bulk up happily in your garden. You will get more pleasure, sometimes for years, from bulbs in your beds and borders than from a few carnations in your drawing room. Many of the species tulips have beautiful leaves, striped in shades of green, white, yellow or red, and their flowers are like bright gems that give a boost of strong colour that is such a fillip in spring.

There are hundreds of species and varieties to choose from, and a good bulb catalogue is one of the best places to look for information on flowering time, heights and to see all the colours. Tiny species will enhance even the smallest flower bed, and they will nestle down among emerging plants like *Brunnera macrophylla*, the giant perennial, whose own huge leaves will hide the disintegrating bulb leaves later. For a burst of colour try *T. praestans* 'Fusilier', which has up to four flowers of flaming scarlet, which will burst up from a carpet of anemones to make a brilliant spring picture.

Other favourites are *T. tarda*, with clusters of up to six flowers from each bulb, which open as soon as the weakest sun shines. Golden yellow petals with pure white tips bring all the romance of central Asian travel to your own garden. In the wild it carpets the slopes of the Tien Shan mountains in Kirghizia and transfers itself effortlessly to the drier edges of our suburban borders.

Nearly all these small bulbs come from high wild places. *T. turkestanica*, which seeds and spreads in stony soil, comes from the slopes of the Pamirs and is a delightful reminder of all the plant collectors who wandered the mountains for us later generations.

Modern plant collectors are still bringing back treasures. One of the best plants to contrast with tiny tulips is the great find by the Compton d'Arcy & Rix 1988 expedition to China that is proving to be an outstandingly good, tolerant and hardy plant. *Corydalis flexuosa* has bright blue flowers over excellent ferny foliage, which is sometimes purple, sometimes a soft green. As well as the species, there are several named forms, of which *C. flexuosa* 'Père David' and 'China Blue' are two already famous and much sought after. It is prolific – one plant can be divided up to make as many as a hundred by the end of the summer – it could become the greatest blue weed of all time.

Tulipa clusiana has been with us for centuries, for it is naturalized in southern Europe although it has spread its fine slender pink and white striped flowers from the Himalayas and Tibet. Plant the bulbs deeply, surround it with the white windflower, *Anemone blanda*, and give it a background of *Euonymous fortunei* 'Silver Queen', with its magnificent cream and green evergreen foliage.

The hybrid tulips in the *Fosteriana* group all came originally from the land between Samarkand and Bokhara, but they are now commonplace in gardening supermarkets. Try *T.* 'Orange Emperor' with the emerging bronze foliage of *Euphorbia griffithii* 'Fireglow' – an amazing summer sight in its own right when in full red flower – and a few bronzed apricot-coloured polyanthus for a colourful corner in a border. The euphorbia will balloon out to make a great dome of foliage to shade the primula and hide the tulip foliage.

A stand of Tulipa '*Orange Wonder*' *is much enhanced by the sword-shaped leaves of* Iris pallida '*Variegata*'.

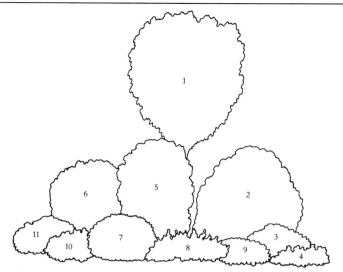

Fig. 2 *Spring-flowering shrubs underplanted with carpets of bulbs.*

1 *Sorbus hupehensis*
2 *Spiraea* 'Arguta'
3 *Lathyrus vernus*
4 *Pulmonaria officinalis* 'Sissinghurst White'
5 *Philadelphus coronarius* 'Aureus' and *Clematis macropetala*

6 *Crambe cordifolia*
7 *Santolina pinnata* ssp. *neapolitana*
8 *Stachys byzantina*
9 *Epimedium* × *youngianum* 'Niveum'
10 *Brunnera macrophylla*
11 *Euphorbia polychroma*

T. 'Purissima' is a pure white form that gleams coolly in a scheme with white hyacinths and *Omphalodes verna* 'Alba', a tiny ground coverer with clusters of lovely white flowers throughout spring. It is also good spearing up through that ground cover *par excellence*, *Gallium odoratum*. This rampant spreader makes mats of foliage and roots, fit to strangle any shrub that gets in the way, but it is worth growing for its fresh green early growth and its spiralling, scented sprays of white flowers. The foliage can be cut and dried, when it smells just like new mown hay, and it was one of the great strewing herbs of medieval England when something sweet-smelling was needed to walk on when all around was stinking.

The gallium looks wonderful under trees and shrubs. Under a *Sorbus hupehensis* (see Fig. 2) it can be easily controlled while making a starry background for early-flowering shrubs. *Philadelphus cornonarius* 'Aureus', with its bright yellow foliage and white flowers against the tiered flowers of *Spiraea* 'Arguta', set with the blue of *Lathyrus vernus* – the archetypal blue pea of spring – and the more robust brighter blue of the brunnera and the delicate, fragile *Epimedium* × *youngianum* 'Niveum', with its tiny white flowers combine to make a symphony of colour. Later, *Crambe cordifolia* is a great star with its cloud of white in early summer to take the border on through the year. The *Sorbus* repeats the story with masses of white berries.

The hybrid *greigii* tulips, which were raised in the 1950s from species, have very bright colour forms. *T.* 'Plaisir' has carmine red petals, which feather into lemon yellow at the edges. As a bonus it has broad red and green striped leaves, which are striking for several weeks. *T.* 'Red Riding Hood', one of the most easily available and popular, has pillar box red flowers with an elegantly waisted shape. Again, the leaves are brilliantly coloured.

From east of Tashkent come the *kaufmanniana* hybrids, which have even more heavily marked leaves and beautiful flowers. They are known as the waterlily tulips because, from tight triangulated buds, they open into wide cups to show their lining colour. *T.* 'Heart's Delight', with its pink and white stripes, is like a robust *T. clusiana*, but it has a pure white heart that makes a striking picture set in a sea of white-flowered *Vinca*.

Most of the species tulips last for only a few days and are then gone for another year, but some of the larger tulips last for weeks, and they are almost more exciting in bud than in flower. When their tall stems and pointed flower buds emerge – always far earlier than you are expecting them if you let them naturalize – they look elegant for weeks before they open. One of the earliest is *T.* 'Apricot Beauty', which will stand up to, but sometimes lean into, the strongest wind. Even when it is curved over, it takes an elegant stance to complement its neighbours. It looks wonderful bending into a large shrub of *Senecio* 'Sunshine', which has bright silver foliage to offset satiny apricot petals. Later, the burgeoning growth of the senecio will hide all trace of tulip leaves.

Fig. 3 *A pink and purple border for colour from spring to late summer.*

1 *Juniperus communis* 'Hibernica'
2 *Kolkwitzia amabilis* and *Clematis* 'Duchess of Albany'
3 *Rosa* 'Blairii Number Two' and *Clematis* 'Lasurstern'
4 *Rosa* 'Mary Rose'
5 *Lavatera* 'Barnsley'
6 *Digitalis purpurea*
7 *Alcea rosea*
8 *Aster novae-angliae* 'Harrington's Pink'
9 *Penstemon* 'Garnet'
10 *Erysimum* 'Bowles' Mauve'
11 *Geranium phaeum*
12 *Aquilegia* double purple form
13 *Berberis thunbergii* 'Atropurpurea Nana'
14 *Polygonum affine*
15 *Epimedium grandiflorum* 'Rose Queen' or *E.* × *youngianum* 'Roseum'
16 *Bergenia cordifolia* 'Purpurea'

Of the mid-season tulips, which flower until late spring, there are two deep purple ones that contrast beautifully with pale pink blossom. *T.* 'Attila' is a rich purple all over and is stunning under *Malus floribunda*, with its cascading pink frill, or with *Kolkwitzia amabilis*, the beauty bush, which bears showers of pink blossom in spring. The kolkwitzia would star in a border alive with pink and purple from spring into late summer (see Fig. 3).

Its spring companions, apart from tulips, could include crocus and narcissus, as well as double purple aquilegias and geraniums, pink epimediums, mauve perennials – try the wallflower *Erysimum* 'Bowles' Mauve' – and, in summer, the kolkwitzia would take the weight of a clematis to draw the eye up to huge shrub roses swagged in pink, with the added bonus of an enormous *Lavatera* 'Barnsley', which would echo the pink and white of *Rosa* 'Blairii Number Two'.

Tulipa 'Arabian Mystery' is also violet-purple, but each petal has a white edge, which gives a lightness that contrasts with and yet reinforces the pristine whiteness of a lovely early flowering shrub, *Exochorda* × *macrantha* 'The Bride', which arches over when heavily laden with bloom.

Double tulips, which look more like peonies than tulips, are indispensable for giving a lush effect when grown in great groups, and their flowers last longer than those of peonies. *T.* 'Mount Tacoma' is a peerless white, with great heads that are wonderfully strong, which lights up groups of winter evergreens. These doubles fit in well with shrub roses, which need space around them to show off their shapes but which have a lot of bare soil on show around before the foliage skirts leaf in spring.

Best of all, however, and easier to grow, are the lily-flowered tulips. These have gracefully reflexed, pointed petals and thin, strong stems. *T.* 'White Triumphator' is without equal among white tulips, and it is a wonder planted into a group of *Brunnera macrophylla*, with its china blue flowers. The tulip starts its journey upwards just as the brunnera's hairy leaves begin to unfurl through the soil. They grow together until the brunnera's bright blue, forget-me-not-like flowers set off the luminous tulip petals. Eventually the brunnera's architecturally moulded leaves engulf and completely obscure the yellowing tulip leaves. Set them under a *Pyrus salicifolia* 'Pendula', which will weep its silver leaves over the scene, and if you are lucky, the *Pyrus* will bear its unspectacular but pretty, white, black-stamened blossom at the same time.

Tulipa 'White Triumphator' always looks good with yellow. Plant some bulbs with *Euphorbia polychroma*, which makes large clumps of rounded foliage set all over with corymbs of acid yellow flowers and which will act as a foil for groups of the white tulip. Add some yellow daisy-flowered leopard's bane, *Doronicum pardalianches*, which has soft, hairy leaves that contrast with the thin, striated euphorbia foliage.

Tulipa 'China Pink', which is a wild rose shade, is enchanting for a pink scheme set about with pink polyanthus and the purple flowers of *Primula* 'Wanda'. Wallflowers are the traditional partners for tulips, but you need space to grow your own from seed to get good plants. The perennial wallflowers are more suitable in many ways because they root easily from cuttings and last as foliage plants – some have bronzed or glaucous leaves – and they live for two or three years. *Erysimum* 'Bowles' Mauve' looks lovely with the pink tulip, but take cuttings every autumn because it often flowers itself to death.

Tulipa 'Burgundy' is a purple lily-flowered tulip. It is very attractive against *T.* 'China Pink' and even better next to groups of *Helleborus orientalis* seedlings, which will have faded to plum and purple by the time the tulips are in bloom. *T.* 'Dyanito' is a sheer, pure scarlet that is strong enough to march out with purples, oranges and yellows in a dramatic clash of colours.

Among the lily-flowered tulips you will find a particularly good cultivar in each colour range. *T.* 'West Point', which has exaggeratedly pointed petals, is the finest yellow. Grow it through yellow sage, *Salvia officinalis* 'Aurea', so that it thrusts through the soft, downy foliage. Accent the yellow glow with a *Lonicera nitida* 'Baggesen's Gold' with its tiny primrose leaves and ferny sweeping growth. For later colour and to make a year-round picture, plant a *Clematis* × *durandii*, which has huge, dark purple flowers, into the ever-gold lonicera. *Ruta graveolens* 'Jackman's Blue' is a useful small shrub to use for spring colour with the lonicera and tulip. It has steely blue, ace-of-clubs shaped foliage with startling white variegation. It looks like the freshest spring flowers and contrasts well with yellow.

One tulip alone sums up the whole of spring – it is called, naturally enough, *T.* 'Spring Green', and it has the coolness and freshness that come at no other time of the year. The thick petals are creamy colour and texture, but they are splashed and blazed with emerald green. Buy as many as you can afford and plant them to drift through a border that peaks in summer rather than spring. The tulips will call all the attention to themselves, and no one will notice that the ground around them is fairly bare.

Most tulips look good growing through another of their traditional companions, *Myosotis*, the forget-me-not, and it used to be a classic practice to plant them in strictly regimented blocks. This seems to be suitable today only for parterre beds where everything is removed two or three times a year and replanted with other short-lived flowers. In a small garden it is much prettier and easier to have a more casual arrangement, with the tulip bulbs grouped in drifts through shrubs and roses and the forget-me-nots allowed to self-seed around to make a footnote for the bulbs. Forget-me-nots are invasive, but they do cover the starkness of bare soil that can make a spring garden look so empty.

If you find it difficult to decide where bulbs should go when they arrive in the autumn, for it is almost impossible to know where the bare spring places will be when fading summer foliage completely covers the ground, and the ground is often too hard to plant bulbs deeply enough, put some or all of them into pots. Keep them carefully in a sheltered place throughout the winter, and then when spring comes you will find it easy to site them just where you need them.

SPRING SHRUBS

Forsythia and flowering currant, *Ribes sanguineum*, with the flowers like hanging raspberries, are the backbone of most spring planting, and they are not to be scorned for they are very colourful.

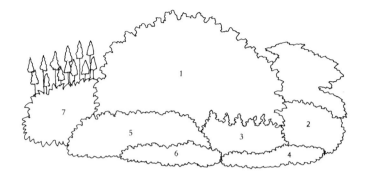

Fig. 4 *A spring planting scheme with bold foliage.*

1 *Physocarpus opulifolius* 'Dart's Gold'
2 *Santolina rosmarinifolia rosmarinifolia*
3 *Lunaria annua* or *L. rediviva*
4 *Viola cornuta* white and blue forms

5 *Anthemis sancti-johannis*
6 *Tanacetum parthenium*
7 *Rodgersia*
8 *Darmera peltata*

An evergreen shrub for any bed or border is *Osmanthus delavayi*, which sprays its elegant foliage out from a dark centre and by mid-spring is covered from head to foot in tiny white, strongly scented flowers. It is one of the great gems found in China at the turn of the century.

All the spiraeas are wonderful spring plants. *Spiraea* 'Arguta' (syn. *S. arguta* 'Bridal Wreath') is one of the best, bringing that purity, sparkle and freshness that epitomizes spring. The starry white blossom is layered along thin arching branches, and once the flowers have gone it is a good shape to take a clematis. *Spiraea japonica* 'Goldflame' is grown for its foliage rather than for its flowers. The leaves appear early, like little red darts on the twigs, and they soon expand into startling gold foliage. The flowers, which are borne in summer, are a purplish-red, and some people cut them off because they clash with the leaves, making the shrub look like a bonfire.

Another good spring shrub is *Physocarpus opulifolius* 'Dart's Gold', which has as good foliage as the spiraea. It is light gold and translucent and looks quite stunning against a dark background. It likes a good soil and will take some shade. Grow it with white tulips (see Fig. 4), and carpet the ground around it with primroses. Add *Santonlina rosmarinifolia*, the green form of cotton lavender, which has entrancing lemon yellow pompon flowers all summer, to accentuate the shrub's foliage. Scads of perennial or annual honesty, *Lunaria annua*, in the white-flowered form, will keep a pristine colour scheme, or let the common mauve flower have its way and enjoy the contrast. Pick up the yellow theme with masses of yellow feverfew, *Tanacetum parthenium* 'Aureum', whose early rosettes of golden foliage are as bright as any flower. The large, impressive foliage of *Rodgersia* and *Darmera peltata* will be an excellent foil.

Thrilling Peonies

One of the great stars of spring is *Paeonia mlokosewitschii*, which sends scarlet buds up through the earth early in spring and then gradually unfurls shrimp pink leaves that have a glaucous blush all over them. The flowers are pure poetry: single translucent cups of pale primrose with large self-coloured stamens. All the drama is over in about ten days, but then you have sculpturally attractive leaves, always tinged with pink, and in the autumn horned capsules split open to reveal scarlet seeds.

Magnolias and Camellias

If the peony is an aristocratic compared with the bread-and-butter shrubs of spring, magnolias and camellias are indeed grandees of the plant world. They are at their majestic best in cool, damp conditions and acid soil, but most gardens can find a home for *Magnolia stellata*, which is slow growing and seldom exceeds 3m (10ft) in height. It is smothered in white star flowers in late spring, and these begin to appear when it is quite a small shrub. *M. stellata* 'Water Lily' is an outstanding form, with larger flowers.

M. × soulangeana takes up quite a wide space, but it will grow almost everywhere. Its huge flower goblets are entrancing seen against a blue sky, and many of the clones have white flowers. *M. × soulangeana* 'Lennei' is one of the best of these – the thick, white petals are rose-purple outside and creamy-white stained with purple inside.

Two other magnolias are worth considering as magnificent centrepieces for a bed. *M. × loebneri* 'Leonard Messel' has lilac-pink flowers, and it will grow on almost any soil, as will *M. × loebneri* 'Merrill', which has large, white, fragrant flowers but is otherwise much the same as 'Leonard Messel' in terms of habit. Although these magnolias are not fussy about soil, remember that in their wild state they are plants of the forest, and a mulch of dead leaves would naturally lie over their roots for much of the year. Try to make well-rotted compost or acquire some leaf mould and apply a mulch around the roots at least twice a year.

Camellias are waxen beauties, perhaps seen at their best in woodland gardens. They can look rather artificial in a flower bed or border, but they can look exquisite in large containers.

STARRY FLOWERS

To complement the bulbs and to run under the great spring shrubs, choose from among the many neat ground-covering plants that will give masses of flower at about the same time. Look out for species that have good year round foliage.

First, for its daintiness and shining leaves, is the epimedium. These plants have heart-shaped leaves on massed wiry stems, and all the species will tolerate some shade. Some have marbled leaves, but all have sprays of tiny flowers in yellows, whites and pinks. They are excellent ground cover under shrubs. The only thing

In late spring the white and pink of that valiant self-seeder red valerian, Centranthus ruber, *foam over an edging of lime green* Alchemilla mollis.

you must do is cut the foliage right down in midwinter, however lovely it is, so that the tiny, starry flowers will not be hidden in the leaves. New gleaming foliage will soon start up to do its pretty year-round trick again.

E. × *versicolor* 'Sulphureum' is the commonest of them all and also the easiest to grow. It will thrive in the driest shade, where its leaves will turn burnished bronze in winter. It has piercing yellow flowers. *E.* × *youngianum* 'Niveum' is a great favourite. The neat clumps of foliage are coloured like milk chocolate in spring, when it is topped by clouds of pure white starry flowers. *Epimedium* × *rubrum* has rosy-tinted leaves and pink flowers. New varieties are coming into commerce all the time, and they may soon become as fashionable as hellebores.

Pulmonarias, lungwort, are also known as spotted dogs for the huge white blotches that cover most of the old varieties' leaves. They are useful spring-flowering plants for shade, and the large, handsome leaves make a strong feature with bulbs and small-leaved plants. The flowers are red, white, blue and pink.

The newer introductions have the most desirable leaves, and one of the most striking is *Pulmonaria rubra* 'David Ward', which was raised by Beth Chatto and named after her propagator. It has exquisite leaves, which are almost entirely silver. In spring they open out into long, wide, whitened blades, and then the plant sends up many stems of startling coral pink flowers. The leaves of *P.* 'Tim's Silver' are nearly as silvery, and they contrast well with the normally spotted varieties. *P.* 'Mournful Purple' has deep purple flowers, *P. officinalis* 'Sissinghurst White' is the best white, and *P.* 'Mawson's Blue' has plain dark green leaves but vibrant dark blue flowers.

All the pulmonarias look good when grown with bergenias, the shining evergreen leaves of which are a fine foil for the roughness of the pulmonaria leaves and the cut leaves of hellebores, which will just be going out of flower as the pulmonarias begin to appear.

The great tribe of euphorbias, with their lime green flowerheads, also bursts forth at this time. *E. amygdaloides* var. *robbiae* sends up dark green rosettes, set about with flat heads of flowers, which gradually swell into large domes of yellow that stay for months.

E. polychroma starts its year in early spring, when succulent leaf buds appear all over the woody basal growth. These gradually expand into a dome of fresh green sprays, each terminating in bright chrome yellow flowers. It stays in good shape until late autumn, when it turns into a mini-bonfire of colour.

The largest and most dramatic of the euphorbias is *E. characias* ssp. *wulfenii*, which is an ornament in the border all through the year, especially in spring, when its huge, lime green heads start to unfurl and then burst into massive heads of hundreds of flowers. It is also the most splendid foliage plant, with narrow, forest green leaves winding up a stem to give a cylindrical effect all year round.

Plant a group of euphorbias surrounded by *Bergenia* 'Bressingham White' for the purity of its flowers and the largeness of its leaves plus several *myrrhis odorata*, the sweet cicely of the herb garden. The *Myrrhis* has huge ferny leaves and umbels of white blossom in spring. These three contrasting foliage plants and their toning flowers will provide a solid architectural centre for airy spring flowers.

CHAPTER 3

SUMMER CORNUCOPIA

IN SOME YEARS THERE is a terrible gap in early summer when the tulips fade fast in bitter winds and the herbaceous plants fail to appear. More often, however, this is a time of great promise in the garden – the bare bones of winter and spring have gone and in their place are the satisfying shapes of green plants, shining with health and bursting with buds yet to unfurl. The beds and borders will soon be swathed in roses, wreathed in climbers and dancing with perennials from all over the world, while annuals, sown in abundance and allowed to self-sow, will fill the gaps left by early bulbs and summer galtonias and lilies race to join the ball. But they all need help.

A fertile soil and high rainfall are perfect for plants, which will root happily and quickly produce luxuriant growth. Most of us, however, have to live with dreadful soil, high winds and too much or too little rain. Our plants need our help in the form of careful feeding, regular watering and mulching if they are to give us the rampantly romantic look that we want. When we provide that care, early summer is the time when we are rewarded by the scent and colour of the first great flush of roses, filling our gardens with colour, scent and grace. At this time, too, irises, delphiniums, peonies, poppies and all other great border plants are at their best.

EARLY PROFUSION

Early summer begins with the rhododendrons and azaleas, which have the most varied colour range of all plants. The species have the most exquisite leaves, with silvery, rusty or furry backs, but they all need acid soil, shelter and high rainfall. They also tend to look best in light woodland, where the ground can be carpeted with bluebells and left to its own devices later in the year, with lilies and hostas used to lighten the gloom of the heavier rhododendron leaves. The best gardens are filled with shrubs that billow and spray and have dramatic leaves. Deutzias, philadelphus, lilacs and weigelas, the great flowering shrubs of early summer, are the backbone of most gardens. They are common because they are good – colourful, hardy, reliable, sweetly scented and beautiful. There are so many different varieties of each there is no need for everyone to have the same, although garden centres tend to provide the easiest and hardiest. It is worth searching for a few that are different.

Lilac, *Syringa*, is a classic of European gardening, but it is rather boring when not in flower, for its heavy green leaves are lifeless and dull. Of course, the pyramids of heavenly scented flower are a must, and for the background of a large bed, *Syringa vulgaris* 'Mme Lemoine', an old double white that flowers for a long time, or 'Souvenir de Louis Spaeth', in wine red and one of the most consistent and reliable flowerers, are unbeatable.

S. vulgaris 'Souvenir de Louis Spaeth' is the basis of a planting scheme in soft pinks, purples and some white. *Allium aflatunense* should throw out its tall spheres of mauve at the same time as the lilac flowers; *A.* 'Purple Sensation' would be even more magnificent, if you can get it. This *Allium* is perfect accompaniment for *Persicaria bistorta* 'Superba', which drapes a carpet of pink spires under the sea of mauve. Add an accent of purple-blue iris, a softening of pink London pride, *Saxifraga × urbium*, and dramatize it all with a planting of white-edged hosta. *Iris pallida* 'Variegata' will give another vertical accent and accentuate the hosta's variegation, while larger shrubs, *Viburnum plicatum*, will bring the roundness of white snowballs to the scene. You could finish off with huge swathes of two great roses – *Rosa* 'Marguerite Hilling' and *R.* 'Cerise Bouquet' – but the scheme is happy without them.

Something Different

For something slightly different try some little known lilacs from Canada, the Prestons hybrids. *S. × prestoniae,* 'Elinor' has dark purple-red buds, which open to pale lavender, and 'Isabella' has purple-pink flowers. They are extremely hardy, have an upright habit, so seem to take up less space than the old fashioned lilacs, and flower profusely in early summer. Isabella Preston, who raised them in Ottawa in 1920, also hybridized the *josiflexa* species to produce *Syringa × josiflexa* 'Bellicent', which is an outstanding clone, unusual and beautiful, with enormous panicles of clear rose-pink flowers.

For a narrow border or small bed, the tiny species lilacs, *S. protolaciniata*, *S. microphylla* 'Superba' and *S. meyeri* 'Palibin' are all pretty, small-leaved shrubs with rosy-lilac, strongly scented flowers, which are borne abundantly in early summer and continue on and off until early autumn. They are lovely for corners or with shrub roses.

Colourful Shrubs

Weigela is good for bulking up a border, for giving showers of pretty blossom at the beginning of the season and for providing a home for a late-flowering clematis. The variegated form, with its fresh cream-and-white splashed leaves, is a wonderful leavener for plain rose foliage. Look out for *Weigela* 'Florida

Clouds of bronze fennel, Foeniculum vulgare *'Bronze', stand behind* Lavandula stoechas *ssp.* pendunculata *and an edging of purple sage.* Allium aflatunense *'Purple Sensation' is the spark that sets the whole scheme alight.*

Variegata' and prune it immediately after flowering to get the best new foliage and to keep it within bounds so that it will grow happily with hardy geraniums and other border flowers. If you need a yellow-flowered shrub to complete a colour scheme, *Weigela middendorffiana*, which has sulphur yellow flowers with dark orange markings, is unusual but slightly difficult. It needs shade and shelter, but when it feels at home it is a great beauty.

Kolkwitzia amabilis, the weigela's cousin, is by far the most aristocratic of these summer flowering shrubs. Known as the beauty bush, it forms an airy fountain of drooping branches draped with masses of bell-shaped, soft pink flowers. Although it grows quite tall, its diaphanous appearance means that it looks wonderful weeping over a small box hedge at the corner of a border of pink and purple roses, poppies and acanthus.

The pearl tree, *Exochorda racemosa*, drips with garlands of white flowers, which look like lustrous pearls. It hates shallow, chalky soils but in the right conditions will grow into a large, free-flowering shrub. Use *Exochorda* as the centrepiece for a colour schemed border (see Fig. 5). It looks superb in a blue, white and yellow scheme, where its short flowering time will be disguised with tiers of planting. The dark evergreen bulk of *Phillyrea angustifolia* will set off the whiteness, which will be accentuated by *Euonymus fortunei* 'Silver Queen', which may take some years to build into a substantial shrub. Hostas can be used to allay any spottiness as they increase into great mounds of ribbed foliage, and herbaceous perennials in the blue range will take the scheme through spring until autumn.

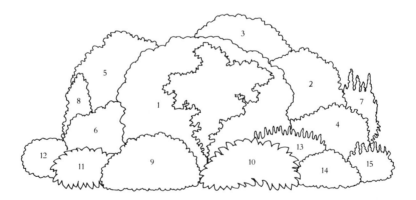

Fig. 5 *A blue, white and yellow border for summer.*

1 *Exochorda racemosa* and *Clematis* 'Prince Charles'	8 *Verbena bonariensis*
	9 *Euonymus fortunei* 'Silver Queen'
2 *Philadelphus coronarius* 'Variegatus'	10 *Hosta sieboldiana*
3 *Phillyrea angustifolia*	11 *Hosta* 'Thomas Hogg'
4 *Campanula lactiflora*	12 *Centranthus ruber* var. *albus*
5 *Buddleia davidii* 'Dartmoor'	13 *Lysimachia clethroides*
6 *Thalictrum delavayi*	14 *Artemisia stelleriana*
7 *Aconitum carmichaelii*	15 *Nepeta* 'Six Hills Giant'

Although it is common most good gardeners agree that one of the best shrubs for gardens all through the year is *Cornus alba* 'Elegantissima', which is a winter wonder with its vermilion stems, but looks even better in summer, when its pale green leaves are margined with creamy white just veiling the redness below. It looks good against a dark hedge, and itself makes a magnificent background for hosts of white or pink *Anemone* × *hybrida*.

PRESENCE AND FORM

Viburnums are a great family of shrubs that are indispensable in the garden. There is a member for every season, some performing well at every season, and all give presence and form to the border. In summer one of the best is *Viburnum plicatum* 'Mariesii', which is like an upturned chandelier. It grows into a fat triangle, with layers of branches, first on one side, then on the other. It has white, flat, lace caps of flower that are spaced along the wide set branches to look like a crinoline decorated with rosettes. Plant three together for a sumptuous luxurious effect massed at the corner of a border or in an island bed, where they can be appreciated from all sides.

Cotoneasters, especially the weeping and trailing ones, elaeagnus, escallonias and hypericums all combine at the height of summer to dress a garden with foliage and flower. The *Elaeagnus* genus includes both evergreen and deciduous species, but all are good garden subjects. In the summer there are few fresher-looking shrubs than the ice-cool foliage of *Elaeagnus commutata*. This has intensely silver leaves with extremely fragrant, although mostly unseen, flowers in late spring. It sometimes produces suckers, which make a little silver forest. It is striking against a yew hedge with white flowers – *Rosa* 'Iceberg', little violas, *Primula* 'White Wanda', the umbellifers *Selinum wallichianum*, with its delicate ferny foliage and off-white blossom of Queen Anne's lace, or *Ammi majus*, an annual with puffy, starred balls of flowers that shine against the silver shrub.

For making lower cushions with almost perpetual flowers, the hypericums and potentillas take some beating. Hypericums are tough, easy plants, which produce round, buttercup yellow flowers with the same sort of buttercup sheen on the petals that make them so seductive. *H.* 'Hidcote' is one of the tallest, with a succession of huge flowers, the largest of any hardy hypericum, which are produced with gay abandon from mid- to late summer.

Hypericum kouytchense is a Chinese rarity, not often seen in gardens. From midsummer onwards it stars in the hot cottage garden at Sissinghurst, where its conspicuously long-stemmed, golden-yellow flowers are freely borne. The bright red, long-style capsules – always a feature, either red or black, in hypericums – resemble colourful upturned stork's heads. Grow it with groups of *Hosta sieboldiana* 'Frances Williams' – the khaki-yellow leaf edges will draw out the colour of the hypericum flowers – and either *Hakonechloa macra* 'Alboaurea', a grass with satiny striped yellow and green leaves, which is sometimes difficult to establish in the ground, although it is easy in pots, or the easier *Alopecurus pratensis* 'Aureus', a grass forming striking low clumps of foliage, vividly striped gold and green.

Another huge family of summer-flowering shrubs is the *Cistus*. They are the prettiest of shrubs for the small garden, and no large garden is complete without a few. The evergreen, often spicily-scented foliage is of many shapes, colours and textures, and the papery flowers, all shades of white through to deepest carmine, appear in prodigious quantity in midsummer. They need a hot, dry spot, and their great advantage is that they are perfect for poor, chalky soils. Some are hardier than others, but all go on and on until a very hard winter cuts them back, but then most will root easily from cuttings.

These sun roses revel in heat. *Cistus* × *hybridus* has crimson-tinted buds, which, as with most *Cistus*, open white. The most dramatic of the genus have purple-blotched flowers, which look stunning when they float over their darkly evergreen leaves. *Cistus* × *cyprius* is one of this type and is very hardy. *C. ladanifer* is taller, up to 2m (6ft) high, and it has chocolate brown basal stains on its petals. *C. laurifolius* is the hardiest species and grows into a large shrub with white and yellow flowers. Clematis will twine happily into its branches and a bright blue *C.* 'Lasurstern' makes a wonderful contrast with the whiteness of the *Cistus*.

Some *Cistus* have pink flowers – *C. parviflorus* is the most beautiful, but it needs a mild climate; *C. purpureus* has large, rosy-crimson, papery flowers, and 'Silver Pink', which is exceptionally hardy, has flowers in long clusters. *C.* × *skanbergii* is one of the prettiest – it has clear pink flowers and delicate pointed leaves, and it is good planted as a group under earlier flowering shrubs.

Deutzias are less common in gardens than some of these shrubs, but they are just as easy to grow. They are ravishingly pretty and, without exception, elegant shrubs. Their delicate flowers, borne in early summer, complement the heavier, blowsy roses. Try *D.* × *elegantissima* 'Rosealind', which is a lovely cultivar with deep carmine flowers. *D.* × *hybrida* 'Magicien' has larger flowers in mauve pink, tipped with white, so that their cascading streams of blossom look like a necklace of garnets. *D. pulchra* has spikes of white flowers like lily-of-the-valley. There are probably fifty varieties to choose from, but very few are available commercially, although some of the best are becoming easier to find now.

PERENNIAL FAVOURITES

Trees and shrubs provide the backbone you need for good shapes and shades in your garden, but herbaceous subjects are the garments with which you decorate the underlying framework. The best perennials have good leaves as well as beautiful flowers, but most are little more than colourful hay. They need to be planted in large drifts across a border or bed to get a spectacular effect. The sculptural species – great thistles like onopordums, the huge-leaved *Crambe cordifolia*, with its enormous heads of white blossom, and the massively architectural cardoons, with their purple heads – can be planted as one-offs, embroidered by their lesser relatives.

There is no such thing as a foolproof perennial, but there are hundreds of easy, reliable plants that come as close to being indestructible as living things are likely to be. The toughest grow into large strong plants, which make a show from the beginning. They are hardy, needing no special protection, fast growing, increase generously without becoming invasive and divide easily to make bigger and better groups if you can afford only one at a time. In addition, most are disease free and do not need to be sprayed. Once they are established they are able to get along without watering and, perhaps most importantly, they bloom for a long time and sometimes more than once in a season.

Japanese anemones, *A. × hybrida*, fulfill all these requirements. Although they are fairly slow to increase, they will romp away in a well-prepared border. It is said you can't be too rich, too thin or have too many anemones. There are many different varieties but among the best is the single white *Anemone × hybrida* 'Honorine Jobert', which has glistening silver cups that stand head and shoulders above their lowlier companions, and even the vine-like foliage looks good on its own. *A. hupehensis* 'Hadspen Abundance', with dark pink, semi-double flowers, is very free flowering; *A. × hybrida* 'Queen Charlotte' is a reliable, late, single pink flowerer, while 'Whirlwind' has very beautiful double white flowers.

The foliage of the Siberian iris, *Iris sibirica*, contrasts well with the anemones, although they flower at different seasons. When you are planning your beds and

Soft pastel shades are planted so that they drift through a large border, backed by a purple-leaved tree. Blue Iris sibirica *brings a vibrant tone to contrast with the pinks of the geraniums, aquilegias, wisteria and, below the container, a tumbling mass of* Saxifraga umbrosa.

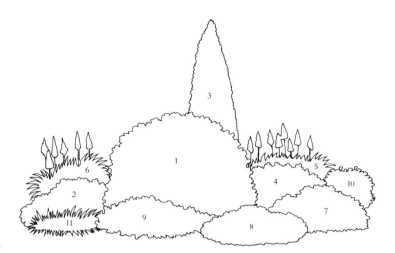

Fig. 6 *Summer planting around a shrub rose.*

1 *Rosa* 'Buff Beauty'
2 *Brachyglottis* Dunedin hybrid 'Sunshine'
3 *Chamaecyparis lawsoniana* 'Columnaris'
4 *Phlomis russeliana*
5 *Iris sibirica* 'Dreaming Yellow'
6 *Kniphofia* 'Ice Queen'

7 *Anthemis tinctoria* 'E. C. Buxton'
8 *Anaphalis margaritcaea* var. *yedoensis*
9 *Alchemilla mollis*
10 *Achillea* 'Moonshine'
11 *Acorus gramineus* 'Oborozuki'

borders, you need to decide if you want things to flower together or at different times to spread the season of interest. Strong leaf shapes, such as the tall, swordlike leaves of the Siberian iris, which look good all the summer unlike those of the bearded iris, will provide a foliage contrast with the anemone. Cultivars of *Iris sibirica* come in many different colours. 'Caesar's Brother' has dark blue flowers; 'Dreaming Yellow' is creamy yellow; 'Limeheart' is a superb white with delicate lime green flower centres; and 'Persimmon' has dark purple flowers. The clumps gradually increase each year and can be divided easily after a few years.

Siberian irises are easier to combine in mixed schemes than the bearded iris, which all too often looks tatty once it has flowered. *Iris sibirica* flowers prolifically and then dies gracefully to leave a fountain of good leaves. *I. sibirica* 'Dreaming Spires' is easy with roses and other herbaceous perennials (see Fig. 6). *Rosa* 'Buff Beauty' trails its great garlands of flower gracefully into the planting, which is made architectural with a stand of *Phlomis russeliana*, with its large, hairy leaves, and *Kniphofia* 'Ice Queen', which has sculptural leaves and exciting towers of flower. *Anthemis tinctoria* 'E.C. Buxton' adds ferny leaves and masses of daisy flowers, while a mound of silvery *Brachyglottis* (syn. *Senecio*) 'Sunshine' and a stand of even whiter *Achillea* 'Moonshine' will help the build up of colour.

The golden marguerite, *Anthemis*, bears hundreds of daisy flowers, which are usually bright yellow, although there is now a white form with a yellow eye. *A. tinctoria* 'E.C. Buxton', which has neat mounds of ferny leaves and creamy-yellow daisies for weeks, is one of best. It grows quite tall – to 60cm (2ft) – but still looks good on the edge of a border, where it will fall forwards gracefully. It takes very easily from cuttings. *A. tinctoria* 'Wargrave' is a brighter yellow and equally good in the border.

The perennial cornflowers are good in early summer when their bright blue flowers make a strong accent in the border. *Centaurea montana* tolerates almost any conditions, divides easily and soon makes a large group. If you cut it down when it has finished flowering, it will make new growth and flower again later in the year.

The campanulas are a wonderful group, which includes both tall, stately back-of-the-border subjects and tiny front-runners to edge a bed. *Campanula persicifolia*, in its single or double forms, is a graceful little plant, which will thread through borders. If it is allowed to seed it will always seem to put itself just where you need it. The bright blue or white translucent bells climb slender stems.

Its larger relatives make tremendous bell towers of blossom. *C. lactiflora*, which grows quickly to 90cm (3ft), has light blue or white flowers, while its relative *C. lactiflora* 'Loddon Anna' has sprays of flesh pink flowers and makes it all the way up to 1.2m (4ft). *C. latiloba* var. *alba* has steeples rather than towers of flowers, but its ghostly presence gleams at the back of wide borders. It grows in the shade and will self-seed prolifically, so beware. *Campanula takesimana*, its lilac-flushed bells spotted with maroon, is a splendid plant, which soon spreads itself to fill a large space.

The intense blue of Campanula persificolia *sparkles with the vivid pink of* Dianthus Highland Hybrids. *The focal point of the group is a cream rose.*

Monarda, known as bergamot or bee balm to cottage gardeners, likes deep, good soil, but it will survive even in a drought, although it will not run around so much. It is sometimes described as invasive, but it is so easy to pull up the runners that it is no hardship. As you pull you will appreciate the strong, minty smell that comes from the leaves. It grows to 90cm (3ft) on strong, square stems, and the flowers are scarlet, pink, white and purple. *M*. 'Cambridge Scarlet' is the old fashioned variety, loved by humming-birds in the United States. The flowers are a soft crimson rather than pillar box scarlet, so do not be frightened to try it. The spectacular hooded flowers, which grow in masses, look quite wonderful when contrasted with white lilies, which will grow up through the masses of pliable roots.

For a really exciting, hot contrast try orange tiger lilies, *Alchemilla mollis* in front and a tall *Achillea filipendulina* 'Gold Plate' behind. The achillea has immense flat flowers, and they will be accentuated if you drop a few corms of *Crocosmia* 'Norwich Canary' – scarlet 'Lucifer' if you feel brave – behind it. The crocosmia has arching stems of pure yellow flowers with a sheen to its petals. Add one of the new English roses, 'Leander', which has pale apricot flowers, or 'Mrs Oakley Fisher' and plant them all in front of a *Cotinus coggygria* 'Royal Purple', with its rounded, gleaming, dark leaves, for a sensational border.

Black-eyed Susan, *Rudbeckia fulgida*, is a daisy that would fit well into that colour scheme to add an even hotter note. *R.F.* var. *sullivanti* 'Goldsturm' has bright yellow petals and a brown cone centre; 'Goldquelle' has double chrome yellow flowers over neat flat leaves.

Day Lilies

In very early spring the day lilies stir into life, and young, curled, fresh leaf tips appear as good as flowers in the dark earth. These make sizeable clumps of wide-bladed grassy leaves. Hybridizers have been very excited by the spectacular flowers that are produced by the *Hemerocallis* genus, and there are so many each year that it has become difficult to tell the difference between them.

The old varieties are still good value if you want yellow and orange. *H. lilioasphodelus* is an early-flowering variety; lemon *H. fulva*, the day lily of the roadsides in America but a much-loved old garden favourite in Britain, is orange. Among new cultivars are the pale lilac 'Luxury Lace', the blush pink 'Catherine Woodbery', which has a lime green eye, and 'Thai Ballet', which has deep pink flowers. All of the cultivars retain a yellowish tinge about their flowers.

MAINTAINING SUMMER COLOUR

Daisy flowers take the border into late summer and keep it colourful. Many gardens run out of steam as summer draws to a close, especially if it has been hot and dry, and this is the time you need clear, bright colours to inject sparkle into the borders. Tall, late-flowering plants are particularly useful for growing in a mixed border. Before they flower, their foliage forms a backdrop for earlier flowers that are situated towards the front of the border. When the taller plants come into bloom they draw the eye up and away from the fading foreground.

Tender plants, such as this vibrant orange dahlia, bring colour to a border in late summer. The glowing shade is accentuated by a drift of bronze Helenium 'Moerheim Beauty' *and orange kniphofias, and lightened by a clump of giant* Leucanthemella serotina *(syn.* Chrysanthemum uliginosum*).*

Among the late-flowering herbaceous plants that will tolerate partial shade are *Achillea ptarmica* 'The Pearl', with its masses of bead-like heads, and pearl everlasting, *Anaphalis triplinervis*, which makes a good edger and has grey foliage. Its larger version, *A. yedoensis*, has brilliant silver foliage, which crunches through the soil as winter ends then throws up chalk white clusters of everlasting daisies that last until late summer.

Heleniums are not rare and unusual, but they are indispensable, indestructible and foolproof. Their golden flowers radiate light at the back of the border in the hottest times of summer. They are bushy plants that can be as tall as 1.8cm (6ft), although most are smaller. The colours range from yellow to red and bronze. One of the finest is 'Moerheim Beauty', which has brown red flowers, and one of the most spectacular is *H.* 'Zimbelstern', which has golden-yellow flowers flecked in brown.

For something far more out of the ordinary try *Macleaya microcarpa* 'Kelway's Coral Plume'. A strong-growing, spectacular plant, it has huge, pink-washed, grey-blue leaves and tremendous heads of coral pink flowers. It can grow up to 2.4m (8ft) or more tall and makes a dramatic foil for late-flowering roses in pink shades.

Oriental poppies, *Papaver orientale*, are dramatic accents for the summer border. They produce great cartwheels of paper-thin petals that surround an amazing heart of black stamens. Most common are the orange and salmon pink forms – 'Sultana', 'Turkish Delight' and 'Curlilocks', for example – but the white forms – 'Perry's White' and 'Black and White' (the black centre is more exaggerated) – are the most beautiful. Good new pale pinks are appearing – 'Cedric Morris' is like a chiffon dress with a grey veiling.

One of the most exciting discoveries for years in the poppy world is *P. orientale* 'Patty's Plum' (syn. 'Mrs Marrow's Plum'). It has the dusky faded coloured bloom of an old plum, and it is much easier to place than the orange monsters. Try it planted towards the middle of a border with a *Rosa glauca* waving overhead – the stem colour almost exactly picks up the poppy petal shading – bronze fennel, to catch the theme and lighten the scheme with its feathery brown leaves, scads of *Sedum* 'Herbstfreude' to surround it, and a neat edging of *Hebe* 'Red Edge' to draw the whole thing together.

One of the huge genus of geraniums, *G. psilostemon* (syn. *G. armenum*) would highlight such a group with its bright, magenta flowers. It is rampant and a huge grower, reaching to 1.5m (5ft) in good soil, and it is attractive from early spring, when its first scarlet shoots appear above ground. It has handsome, scalloped foliage, followed by the stunning flowers, and the plants quickly seed themselves among the shrubs and other perennials.

No bed or border is complete without a geranium or two. The species and varieties cover the whole spectrum of colours, from almost black to white, and not only do they have good ground-covering leaves but they are very tough. They range from the very tall, like *G. psilostemon*, to the tiniest edgers. Among the most beautiful is *G.* 'Johnson's Blue'. The sky blue petals look perfect planted at the front of a border with groups of silver artemisias, especially *A. stelleriana*, which has white foliage that looks as if it has been cut out of felt. The thick violet blue flowers of *G.* × *magnificum* are good under trees, and it has lovely leaves. *G.* 'Ann Folkard' is rampant, but it has delicious yellowy leaves and bright magenta-purple flowers.

There are double geraniums in blue, and white ones for shade or sun; there is the almost black one, *G. phaeum* 'Mourning Widow', and the weed-smothering *G. macrorrhizum* – look out especially for the white form with scented leaves, which even tolerates dry shade. Then there is *G.* × *oxonianum* 'Wargrave Pink', which is one of the most floriferous of all perennials. The pale pink flowers first appear in early summer with the roses, and the flowers will weave around the roses to help to disguise their bareness, flowering until midsummer. Cut it down at that stage, and it will continue to reward you with flowers throughout the autumn.

Candles of Flower

Add a touch of distinction and difference to your beds and borders by including some of those plants that bring candles of colour throughout the whole summer. Try lysimachias, or loosestrife, especially *L. ephemerum*, which bears tall, white spires of flower; *Knautia macedonica*, with its deep red scabious-like flowers; and *Morina longifolia*, which has soapy evergreen thistle leaves and whorls of pink flowers. You should also look out for the new regiments of salvias, which are now being introduced to gardeners from such far-flung places as China and America, and the thalictrums, with their tall heads of purple, white and lavender fluff.

Phlox in all their many colours are among the loveliest flowers of the summer provided mildew does not spoil them. They are at their very best in midsummer, and they do well in sun or semi-shade, where they will not dry out. *Phlox paniculata* comes in many colours, ranging from white to dark violet. Combine a plain pink variety of *Phlox paniculata* with *Lychnis coronaria*, studded with its strong cerise flowers, to create one of the showiest sights of the late summer. Add *Phlox paniculata* to *Lythrum salicaria* 'Firecandle', with its immense spears of magenta, and soften the overall effect with a large shrub of *Ceanothus* × *delileanus* 'Gloire de Versailles', which has fluffy powder blue flowers, and finish this combination off with the steely blue, rounded heads of *Echinops ritro* to make a strong contrast with the phlox.

Hosta Fever

Some plants have become so popular in the last few years that whole beds and borders are devoted to them. Hostas and grasses are two such, and they certainly do go well together. However, they look even better when they are planted among other perennials.

Hostas come in a huge variety of sizes and colours. The tiny ones – for example, *H.* 'Ginko Craig', which has small, lance-shaped leaves with white margins, and *H.* 'Golden Prayers', which has superb golden leaves and a dwarf habit – form flat mounds that are just right at the edges of beds. Most exciting are the huge varieties of hosta. *H.* 'Sum and Substance' has massive leaves, *H.* 'Zounds' has a puckered golden foliage that forms a gigantic pile in time, and *H.* × *sieboldiana* 'Big Daddy' has large tucked blue foliage, which makes a wonderful accent when planted in a striking border of blue geraniums, *Viola cornuta*, with its tiny blue pansy flowers, together with tall, soaring campanulas and a group of *Rosa* 'Felicia'.

The 'blue' hostas, with their glaucous leaves and pale lavender or white flowers, make a lovely fringe for a narrow border where, perhaps *Rosa* 'New Dawn' is planted on a wall above. The great crinkled leaves of *H. sieboldiana*, one of the famous old hostas, are grey-blue with a delicate bloom and are deeply veined. They always look magnificent planted with a group of old fashioned pink roses or under trees where they like the shade. Give them a tall white iris, perhaps *Iris* 'White City', whose sword-like leaves contrast wonderfully with the rounded mounds of hosta.

Fig. 7 *A white and silver scheme for midsummer.*

1 Pots of white pelargoniums, marguerites, *Argyranthemum frutescens*, and *Tulipa* 'Mount Tacoma'
2 *Buxus sempervirens*
3 *Cynara cardunculus*
4 *Deutzia × magnifica*
5 *Ligustrum ovalifolium* 'Argenteum'
6 *Ammi majus*
7 *Physostegia virginiana* 'Summer Snow'
8 *Nepeta racemosa* 'Snowflake'
9 *Anaphalis triplinervis* 'Summer Snow'
10 *Epimedium × youngianum* 'Niveum'
11 *Miscanthus sinensis* 'Variegatus'
12 *Elymus hispidus*
13 *Centaurea cineraria* ssp. *cineraria*
14 *Rosa* 'Iceberg'
15 *Artemisia* 'Powis Castle'

White and Silver

White and silver schemes are always cool and soothing in the sea of yellow daisies that are the mainstay of the late summer garden. If you have no room for a garden of white flowers among great green yew hedges, a section of border can make a calming interlude. Such a section often looks best when it is placed in the centre of a border or at the front of a bed.

Cynara cardunculus, the great silver cardoon, makes a magnificent centrepiece for such a scheme (see Fig. 7). Use pots and containers for a selection of tender flowering plants and emphasize them with two box balls, one on each side. Use white 'Iceberg' roses to balance the design and fill in any gaps with perennials with contrasting foliage shapes and textures.

Some perennials enhance other plants by casting their hazy flowers and foliage across large blooms. *Verbena bonariensis* has tall slender stems, which may reach 1.5m (5ft), but it is so delicate that its tiny lavender blue flowers are no more than a veil when seen with roses. One of its best companions is the large *Gypsophila paniculata*, whose billowing clouds of white blossom enhance the blue fragility. G. 'Rosy Veil' which grows to only around half the size of the species, is an excellent pale pink cultivar for the front of the border.

The ethereal, lacy white tiers of Cornus controversa *'Variegata' literally float above a carpet of foliage and flowers, accentuated by hostas and pink* Persicaria bistorta *'Superba' (syn.* Polygonum bistorta *'Superbum').*

Poker Flowers

Some of the kniphofias flower early in the summer, but most of these tall poker flowers peak in midsummer and do their fiery best throughout late summer. They look dramatic set among low-growing plants, but they are even better with grasses. Many of them live up to their common name of red-hot poker, especially cultivars such as 'Fiery Fred', which has brilliant orange red spikes. This looks especially striking when interplanted with the dark red *Euphorbia dulcis* 'Chameleon', which has rich purple foliage and yellow-green flowers. Add a grass like *Deschampsia cespitosa* 'Gold Veil', which has golden-bronze blades with elegant silver-green flowers that fade to yellow and form a fine-gauzed veil to shimmer over the kniphofia. Tuck in a few bulbs of *Lilium henryi*, which will arch gracefully as their apricot flowers come out; they will increase to grow up through the frail structure of the grass.

Kniphofia 'Bressingham Comet', which has yellow to flame red spikes in autumn, was introduced by Alan Bloom who first made the idea of interplanting kniphofias with grasses fashionable. His idea of planting 'Bressingham Comet' with *Stipa tenuissima* has been copied many times, and it is the perfect focal point for a bed of yellow-leaved hostas, *Stachys byzantina* 'Primrose Heron' with its furry yellow leaves, and a backing of *Foeniculum vulgare*, fennel, with its starry umbels of lime green flowers and its feathery foliage. *Stipa tenuissima* is a grass of ethereal beauty as its flower spikes fray in wind and weather and wrap themselves around the kniphofia.

Many of the new kniphofias have slender spikes of flower that provide a happy contrast with the rounds of other late summer flowers. *K.* 'Modesta' has unusual creamy-white spikes, which develop from apricot pink buds in late summer, while *K.* 'Ice Queen' is much taller with dramatic large spikes of green flowers, which gradually turn to cream as autumn approaches. Prettiest of all these spiky subjects is *K.* 'Little Maid', which has neat, narrow foliage topped with ivory white flowers that appear at the very end of summer and last into autumn.

Late Summer Stand-bys

Nowadays almost every gardener who wants colour late in the summer seems to have planted *Lavatera* 'Barnsley'. It is a shrubby plant that is smothered with pale pink, almost white, flowers that have a bright pink eye. It starts to flower in midsummer and just goes on and on, with even bad weather hardly affecting the profusion, until the first frosts turn the blooms to pathetic brown scraps. It needs trimming in the spring to get it into shape, for it is a wild grower, throwing out huge, pliable stems that will overwhelm slighter subjects in the border.

The lavatera goes supremely well with that other late summer stand-by, *Buddleia davidii*. These shrubs produce many tapering heads of soft blues, purples, mauve pinks and whites. *B.* 'Lochinch' is a good variety; it has tiny lavender blue flowers set into silvery foliage. Another favourite is *B. davidii* 'Dartmoor', which has pendant tassels of bright blue-mauve flowers rather than stiffly upright clusters. 'Dartmoor' looks particularly good with hydrangeas and hardy fuchsias, forming a group will take the garden colourfully into autumn.

Hydrangea paniculata 'Kyushu' has unusual cone-shaped blooms in white; *H. arborescens* 'Annabelle' has great domes of transparent greeny-white petals and *H. macrophylla* 'Blue Wave' has the most beautiful lace-caps of single flowers arranged in rays.

The mop-head hydrangeas come in the blue, pink and white shades that are desperately needed at the end of summer. *H. serrata* 'Preziosa' is a good deep red; *H. macrophylla* 'Hamburg' and *H.m.* 'Westfalen' are in the pink-red range. All need good, deep, moisture-retentive soil and it needs to be acid if you want to keep any variety that peculiar China blue that *H. macrophylla* 'Générale Vicomtesse de Vibraye' will flaunt if the soil is right.

There are so many good herbaceous border plants, some of great refinement, and many more difficult to grow than those mentioned above that the problem lies in discovering them. Visit a garden open to the public, a good nursery or garden centre and study the catalogues. You will want them all.

LATE BULBS

Lilies will enhance the delicacy of frothy plants like gypsophila. It is often best to plant the bulbs in pots in the autumn when you receive them from the merchant and to overwinter them in a sheltered place. Then, when they come into leaf or flower, you can see exactly where to place them in a bed or border. If you prefer, keep them in pots, placing the plastic ones in which you have grown them inside an ornamental terracotta pot. When they have flowered, set them in the ground exactly where they will complement the roses or perennials in years to come.

Lilium regale is one of the cheapest and easiest to grow. It is a strong grower and will usually naturalize once it is planted in the ground. It looks and smells magnificent. Group it with 'Iceberg' roses and add a touch of gypsophila for one of the coolest pictures of summer. If you need a pink lily *L.* 'Pink Perfection' is without peer. It grows to 1.8m (6ft) tall and has immense, dusky pink trumpets, yet it has a simplicity that looks right even in a cottage garden border. Many of the lillies are fairly formal-looking flowers – 'Casa Blanca' and 'Casa Rosa', for instance – and they need careful placing to look right.

The genus *Allium* includes some of the most unusual and exciting flowers of early summer, yet few people know about them. They are members of the same family as the ordinary onion, and, in fact, they look just like onions gone to seed, except that the flowers are the most exotic colours – purple, bright pink and deepest blue. *Allium aflatunense* is one of the easiest to obtain and to grow. Just put the large white bulbs into the ground in groups in autumn, or put them in pots if you are not certain quite where you will want them to appear in summer. In early summer tall drumsticks will shoot out from the ground followed shortly by large balls of blue flowers. They last well and self-seed readily. Even more dramatic than the species is *A. aflatunense* 'Purple Sensation', which flowers slightly later and, when planted in groups across the middle of a mixed border, will highlight drifts of dianthus, polemoniums and aquilegias. Most spectacular of all is *A. christophii* (syn. *A. albopilosum*), which has large heads, 15–40cm

(6–16in) across, but that are light and delicate as if made of filamented steel supporting star-shaped lilac flowers. All these alliums are perfect foils for old fashioned roses, violas and silver-foliaged plants.

Allium karataviense causes quite a stir when its leaves show through in late spring. They are broad, grey-green striped with maroon, and above them appear dense umbels of whitish flowers, just tinged with rosy lilac. Place them near the front of a border because they are only about 20cm (8in) high. The bluest of all is *Allium caeruleum* (syn. *A. azureum*), a handsome, tall-growing species with deep blue flowers. It needs to be planted in groups for it is a slight grower, unlike the others, which have stout, strong stems.

A distinct and unusual species is *Allium nigrum*, which has many globular heads of white florets. It flowers in midsummer, later than all the others, and its cool-looking blooms are lovely with the yellows that predominate in the mixed border. It is even better with drifts of white nicotiana and *Salvia argentea*, which has enormous silkily felted leaves of pure silver.

CLEMATIS

The late summer, when many flowers have finished for the year but asters, chrysanthemums and kniphofias are yet to come, can be enlivened with clematis. Do not grow them as wall shrubs, but allow them to sprawl over shrubs and roses that have become boring. The *viticella* hybrids are the easiest to establish in a mixed border in this way, and they give the longest succession of bloom. They have to be well fed and watered to flower over such a long period, but they repay all your hard work. Clematis wilt, the disease that sometimes afflicts large-flowered clematis, seems to leave the *viticellas* alone.

C. viticella was introduced into England during the reign of Queen Elizabeth I, and it was commonly known as the virgin's bower. Since then it has been hybridized and improved until today there is an enormous range of them. Rather than large flowers, most of the *viticellas* have a mass of tiny ones, borne over a long period and well into early autumn. They make marvellous companions for shrubs, roses and perennial border plants.

C. viticella 'Purpurea Plena Elegans' was one of the earliest varieties in cultivation and it must have caused quite a stir when it first appeared. It has the most extraordinarily good flowers – they are large, double, purple rosettes, 4–6cm (1½-2½in) across, covered in the most elaborate arrangement of frills. They cover the great vines that build up, and even though it is cut back almost to the ground in early spring, long, twining stems soon extend up into trees, across roses and will even cover a large apple tree. They need a light background if they are to be seen to best advantage. A dark conifer will absorb the rich purple colour and the clematis will become almost invisible. A deciduous tree or a large shrub rose, with pink or white flowers, would be much more suitable.

The modern *viticellas* have a wonderful colour range. The most delicate is 'Alba Luxurians', which has nodding white bells. 'Etoile Violette' has dark violet petals with magnificent white stamens, and 'Polish Spirit' has deep purple flowers in huge clusters.

The long, hot days of high summer enhance the beauty of Clematis viticella *'Abundance' as it weaves through the red-leaved* Berberis × ottawensis purpurea.

They can be used in beds or borders in dozens of ways. They climb happily through roses and can even be planted into the same hole as a new rose. Both like the same conditions – plenty of food and water – and the clematis can be cut back when the rose is pruned. Planted in the mixed border, just like an herbaceous perennial, the vines will climb up any neighbouring shrub and roam over the other plants. Avoid the vigorous cultivars for this sort of operation, and try instead the deep red 'Kermesina', creamy-bluish-white 'Little Nell', the white, purple-veined 'Minuet', rosy pink 'Margot Koster' and the purple, white-veined 'Venosa Violacea'.

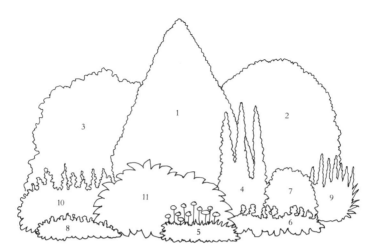

Fig. 8 *Small shrubs interwoven with* Clematis *'Gipsy Queen'*.

1 *Taxus baccata* Aureo group
2 *Lonicera nitida* 'Baggesen's Gold'
3 *Choisya ternata* 'Sundance'
4 *Digitalis purpurea* f. *alibflora*
5 *Allium christophii*
6 *Bergenia* 'Silverlight'
7 *Aster* × *frikartii* 'Mönch'
8 *Veronica prostrata* 'Trehane'
9 *Sisyrinchium striatum* 'Aunt May'
10 *Penstemon* 'Sour Grapes'
11 *Hosta siebolidana* 'Frances Williams'

C. 'Madame Julia Correvon' is a very strong grower, which looks beautiful growing into *Rosa glauca*. Other large shrub roses that flower only once can be decorated with a *viticella* so that they are adorned with flowers into autumn. Clematis love the rangy, strong stems of roses like 'Fritz Nobis' and 'Mme Lauriol de Barny', which are rather dull when they are out of flower. Lilacs, too, take easily to this regime, and a light-flowered *C. viticella* like 'Pagoda', with its reflexed petals, looks delightful against the dull leaves of the shrub.

An ideal small group of shrubs for clematis weaving are yew and shrubby lonicera (see Fig. 8). *Clematis* 'Gipsy Queen' is very floriferous, and the rich purple blooms look brilliant against the yellow of *Lonicera nitida* 'Baggeseus Gold' and golden yew. Light the scheme with bulbs and perennials in the violet and white ranges. *Veronica prostrata* 'Trehane' is a particularly effective yellow-foliaged edger that has intensely blue flowers in summer. *Penstemon* 'Sour Grapes', in subtle shades of blue and green, looks wonderful against the lonicera all summer.

PEERLESS PENSTEMONS

Penstemons used to have a reputation for being tender, but they are now back in favour as gardeners have come to realize that they are easy to propagate from

Dark red sedums, dahlias and Penstemon *'Garnet' are somewhat tender, but their vibrant colours add excitement to the summer border.*

cuttings. It is certainly worth taking a little trouble with them because the flowers are so beautiful. Most of the first specimens to be introduced to Europe were collected in America in the last century, and they found instant favour with Victorians who had the staff to look after and propagate them.

Today there is nothing quite like penstemons for bringing colour and excitement to the late summer garden. Although original plants will rarely survive most winters, cuttings taken in autumn and over-wintered will soon bulk up in the garden. Plants give their best display in their second year after they have been cut back to about 7.5cm (3in) to encourage the formation of vigorous flowering stems. Cut back in late spring for the best results.

P. 'Garnet' is one of the hardiest and easiest. It has narrow, strong red blooms on many thin stems that rise up from the basal growth. P. 'King George' is larger in all its parts and slightly softer in colour. In pink there are P. 'Osprey', 'Apple Blossom' and 'Hidcote Pink'. P. 'Alice Hindley' and P. 'Stapleford Gem' are excellent in the blue-mauve range, while P. 'Sour Grapes', which has flowers bunched together just like grapes, is especially distinctive.

Only one white penstemon seems to be widely available, and it is known prosaically as P. 'White Bedder'. It is not very hardy, and cuttings should be taken without fail if you want to have constant supplies of its pure white flower in late summer. The 'black' penstemons are the newest and most exciting – they liven up a pink and white scheme, and add depth to a purple one. P. 'Charles Rudd', P. 'Raven', P. 'Blackbird' and P. 'Merlin' are the ones to look out for – they have a dark sheen that looks excellent grouped with roses of any colour.

THE TIME OF ROSES

It is all too easy to be seduced by roses. The specialist catalogues are enough to inspire one to order such historic varieties as 'Ispahan', with it exquisite half-open blooms of lovely clear pink, 'Mme Hardy', the most beautiful white rose with a green eye, and the stripy York and Lancaster Rose, *R.* × *damascena versicolor*. They are almost impossible to resist, but they can be over-planted. Those rose-smothered gardens that are superb in early summer with the colour and scent of old fashioned and shrub roses are too often over four weeks later.

It is true that roses on their own in beds or borders produce great banks of colour, usually very bright, for three months of the year, but for the rest of the year they are nothing more than bundles of stiff, ungainly sticks. Some people still prefer to grow their roses in this way so that they can be fed frequently, dead-headed every day and sprayed non-stop. But this is no way to have colourful beds and borders throughout the year.

Some roses mix very well in a bed or border devoted to shrubs and herbaceous perennials. They grow happily with bulbs, which have mostly disappeared below ground by the time the rose comes into its own. And they are highlighted by the late summer bulbs – galtonias, lilies and even species gladioli.

The new, more graceful but floriferous roses are increasing in number every year. Planted in traditional rose gardens with nepeta (catmint) as a blue edging and interwoven with cottage garden pinks, violas and coloured primroses for early colour, they can be planted in shades of pink, lilac, crimson, purple and mauve to make a traditional but continuous scheme.

At a garden in Northamptonshire, in Britain, Anne Huntington, an American, has translated the traditional English rose garden into her own idiom. In a garden paved with stone she has made circles of beds in which two varieties in each shade are planted together to make a swirling melange of soft colour that lasts for months. Each flower has been carefully picked for form, scent and its repetitive qualities.

A few of these roses are 'musts' for a mixed border. 'Mary Rose', double pink flowers, looks rather like an old Damask rose, but it is always branching to make new shoots and new flowers. 'Graham Thomas' is perhaps the best, although it is deep, strong yellow, a colour never found in the old roses. It has upright, bushy growth and it is very vigorous. The excellent foliage never seems to get black spot or rust, even when it is never sprayed, and it is utterly beautiful in bud and flower. Its only fault is its vigour, which means that a strong wind will knock it sideways. Provide a strong stake to hold it up, or, better still, support it among shrubs and trees. It makes a magnificent picture planted in front of a group of thujas – conifers with shining olive green foliage – with a yellow hop, *Humulus lupulus* 'Aureus', twined up into them, a *Buddleia davidii* 'Dartmoor', with its huge trusses of blue blossom, on one side to support the rose and a *Lavatera thuringiaca* 'Ice Cool', with its stout, fan-like growth and its flat, shimmering flowers to contrast and hold it, on the other. In front try hostas in the yellow-green range for architectural foliage, with grasses like *Stipa tenuissima* to shimmer nearby and *Stachys byzantina* 'Primrose Heron' with its soft furry leaves tinged with yellow, to contrast. A mixture of apricot coloured *Lilium* 'African Queen' lilies with *L.* 'Connecticut King' can be added to give strength to the overall colour harmony.

All beds and borders need to make a statement and one very large rose that has good foliage and shape can do it beautifully. *Rosa* 'Alba Semiplena', sometimes thought to be the White Rose of York and certainly one of the roses that dates back to the Middle Ages and possibly beyond, has clusters of large, flat, single, milk-white flowers with golden stamens, which appear for about six weeks on a fountain of grey-green foliage that has a delicate beauty all its own. It grows upwards and can be staked to make a good centrepiece for a border of white flowers and herbs.

R. 'Constance Spry' would make a more formal statement. This is one of the most desirable and one of the first of the newer English roses. It, too, flowers only once, but they are huge, and magnificent pink blooms, with a luminous delicacy that is almost unique, and they smell strongly of myrrh. It is a big plant, but it can be manipulated to keep its place in the border with strong stakes and secured with rope.

The genuinely old roses – the famous *Rosa mundi* with its irresistible but mildewy stripes, the apothecary's rose, *R. gallica* var. *officinalis*, with its muddled flowers, and 'Tuscany Superb', which has the darkest maroon-crimson flowers with gold stamens – can all be fitted in with shrubs. Tucked into the weigelas and deutzias they run into them and their flowers decorate another's branches for their short lives.

Rosa mundi fits well into a mixed border (see Fig. 9). Thread a *Clematis viticella* over its busy growth to flower after the roses have faded and add groups of lavender with good rounded shapes, irises to make interesting vertical shapes, dianthus, to make a glaucous footing, and the pinks and purples of geraniums and linarias to flower in later summer. Yet another clematis on a tripod makes an architectural but flowery accent.

There are damask roses, like 'Ispahan' and 'Gloire de Guilan' with huge pink flowers and beautiful scent; there are the great *albas* like 'Maiden's Blush' and 'Köningin von Dänemark', both of which have soft pink flowers and 'Köningin von Dänemark' looks as if raspberry juice was stroked over the petals; and *centifolia* roses like 'Tour de Malakoff' a rich, sumptuous beauty in parma violet, and 'Fantin-Latour', which is charming again in pink and well deserving its famous name.

Then there are the moss roses. Try 'Soupert et Notting', with moss-covered

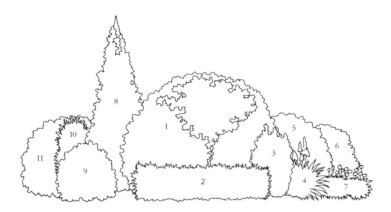

Fig. 9 *A violet, pink and white scheme for large shrubs and roses.*

1 *Rosa mundi* and *Clematis viticella* 'Alba
  Luxurians' or 'Gillian Blades'
2 *Lavendula angustifolia* 'Hidcote'
3 *Knautia macedonia*
4 *Iris* 'Broadleigh Peacock'
5 *Clematis integrifolia*

6 *Rosa* 'Yvonne Rabier'
7 *Dianthus* 'White Ladies'
8 *Clematis* 'Etoile Violette' (grown on a tripod)
9 *Malva moschata*
10 *Linaria purpurea*
11 *Geranium psilostemon*

buds opening into deep pink flowers covering its neat but small body. 'William Lobb' is one of the best moss roses, but it is tall and robust. Plant it at the back of a border where it will fall forward to mingle with other shrubs. Also known as 'Old Velvet Moss', it opens dark crimson fading to a violet-grey.

For tiny, delicate growth, to contrast with the hugeness of 'William Lobb', the China roses are perfect. On their own they can star in the narrowest border or at the front of bigger beds, where they will flower on and off all through the summer. Do not expect masses of bloom, but they have a delicacy and refinement that is just like a Chinese silk painting. 'Hermosa' is small, twiggy and starred with tiny pink flowers like little globes. *R.* × *odorala* 'Mutabilis' has fragile growth, which takes time to build up, but it will grow up and into shrubs, and its blooms are almost continuous. Pointed, flame-coloured buds open to coppery-yellow single flowers that change to pink then coppery-crimson.

Of the Portland roses, 'Madame Knorr' (syn. 'Comte de Chambord') is the most beautiful. It flowers almost without cease through the summer, the full-petalled blooms opening flat and quartered. It is the rose that typifies summer with its scents and warm colours. Grow it in groups of three for the best effect and mass hardy *Geranium* × *oxonianum* 'A.T. Johnson' at his feet with an edging of lavender, *Lavandula angustifolia* 'Hidcote', with its dark purple spikes.

When it comes to choosing between the bourbon roses, it is quite easy to see how a garden can become overloaded with roses. 'Louise Odier' is the flower of dreams, with its cupped pink flowers softly shaded with lilac. 'Mme Isaac Pereire' has huge madder-crimson flowers, a rich fragrance and a magnificent flower shape. It flowers well in summer, but the flowers are better shaped in autumn. 'Bourbon Queen', an old cottage favourite, blends well with other border flowers with its scumbled pink petals and delicious scent. 'Mme Lauriol de Barny' has large, double, pale pink flowers and makes a huge, weaving shrub that grows well with lilac.

'Blanche Double de Coubert' is the perfect shrub rose. It is studded with flat white roses all summer, it has healthy clean foliage, and it grows into a tall, gracefully arching shrub without any staking, and will stand up to the roughest weather. Combine it with hummocks and cushions of *Geranium clarkei* 'Kashmir White', *Iris sibirica* 'Flight of Butterflies', with rich blue flowers veined with white for a spiky contrast, and twine a *Clematis viticella* 'Blue Boy' for its nodding dark blue heads to contrast with the rose in late summer.

All-white schemes often feature 'Blanche Double de Coubert' (see Fig. 10). Try it flanked by *Lavatera thuringiaca* 'Ice Cool' to accentuate the papery whiteness of the rose, with campanulas and lychnis at waist height, and a froth of white geraniums, aquilegias and hellebores at different seasons around the base. If you use lilies, galtonias and snowdrops, this white scheme will last from late winter through spring into late summer.

The hybrid musks bear flowers in large trusses like a floribunda, but they have long, graceful wands of flower and soft colours. 'Buff Beauty' is always worth including in a garden. It has good red-tinged stems and leaves on lovely branches

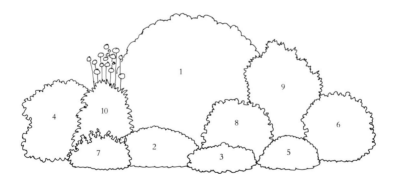

Fig. 10 *A white border for midsummer.*

1 *Rosa* 'Blanche Double de Coubert'
2 *Lavatera thuringiaca* 'Ice Cool'
3 *Helleborus orientalis* white form
4 *Campanula latifolia* var. *alba*
5 *Lychnis coronaria* 'Alba'
6 *Geranium sylvaticum* 'Album'
7 *Aquilegia vulgaris* var. *alba*
8 *Thalictrum aquilegiifolium* var. *album*
9 *Artemisia lactiflora*
10 *Anemone* × *hybrida* 'Whirlwind'

all the year, and then exciting corymbs of buds appear early and hang down in great numbers. The flowers open slowly and last for many weeks, with a few later in the autumn. Grow it against a dark background, allowing it to weave through a yellow-foliaged conifer where its dark foliage shows up well. At its base plant *Euphorbia polychroma*, with its mounds of bright yellow flowers and tiny narrow foliage, and next to it the plant that goes with everything, *Alchemilla mollis*, with its scrolled leaves that are crimped at the edges and its luxuriant sprays of lime green flower. *Brachyglottis* (syn. *Senecio*) 'Sunshine' will add a touch of silver foliage, and as a final touch, place some large pots of white petunias into the alchemilla to give it all an edge.

'Felicia', 'Penelope' and 'Moonlight' are other hybrid musks that flower profusely in early summer and then repeat the performance at least once more during late summer and autumn. 'Felicia' is the pink to have, because its silvery

Rosa 'Cornelia', a hybrid musk, flowers for months above a carpet of Viola cornuta *and edging domes of lavender.*

sheen adds a glow to any border. 'Penelope', which has cream flowers with a pink tinge, grows outwards and downwards to weave into a group of shrubs and other roses. It looks particularly attractive sweeping over low box balls on the corner of a border with R. 'Marguerite Hilling', the pink form of 'Nevada' throwing a canopy overhead. To top the whole group, R. 'Cerise Bouquet' can be used to throw huge, strong growths 3m (10ft) into the air, to cascade down with the weight of its bright cerise, furled flowers that start to appear in midsummer and go on and on into autumn. *Clematis* 'Perle d'Azur' with its sky blue white-stamened flowers should be planted with R. 'Penelope' to climb up through the whole group for a symphony of colour.

R. 'Moonlight', another hybrid musk, will grow very tall if you let it, and its semi-double, creamy-white flowers that are produced in enormous trusses will grow happily at the back of a border, where its mahogany coloured stems and dark green foliage makes a stunning background for its spectacular flowers. Like all the hybrid musks, it can be pruned hard to keep it neat and tidy for a traditional rose bed scheme. Disciplined, it can be used with a clipped box, santolina in its silver and green forms, and mounds of different hostas – glaucous blue, striped with yellow or primrose pale – for a subtle scheme with contrasting foliage and flower.

R. 'Nevada' and R. 'Frühlingsgold' are two modern shrub roses that produce the first summer blooms on large lax shrubs. They both have flat faces with large golden stamens – 'Nevada' is white, 'Frühlingsgold' yellow – and both are exceptionally graceful with arching branches that are as elegant as any once flowering shrub. They are perfect hosts for clematis, and a host of other perennials, especially hostas and hellebores, can be grown under their canopies.

'Maigold' is a shrub rose that makes a great mound of shining bronze-touched foliage. It is often the first rose to flower, and it is said to smell of coconut. The delightful flowers are pale apricot and yellow, with huge golden stamens. It is very prickly, but it is exceptionally tough and hardy, and its branches can be pulled down so that flowers bloom all along their lengths. Grow it at the side of a deep border where its rather angular base can be covered with something rampant like *Vinca major* 'Variegata', which is a powerful ground cover with magnificently blotched and patched yellow foliage. Its bright blue flowers often appear at the same time as those of 'Maigold'. As it often features in a big border, it needs large groups of perennials and shrubs to give it a grounding in a border. *Bupleurum fruticosum* will make a good sea green background laced with lime green flowers after the rose has faded.

Rosa 'Ballerina', R. 'Bonica' and R. 'The Fairy' are very different from R. 'Maigold'. All three are neat, small bushes with excellent pink flowers, and all are perfect for a small bed. 'Ballerina' has huge clustered heads of tiny single flowers that last all summer. 'Bonica' is perhaps the best of the newer small shrub roses; unusually for a rose, it has a lovely shape, making a large, green dome that is covered with masses of flowers that appear in sprays. It flowers almost all the time and looks best over a carpet of *Gypsophylla paniculata* 'Compacta Plena', which has fluffy clouds of delicate pink flowers over grey foliage. 'The Fairy' is

The arching stems of shrub rose R. 'Frühlingsgold' make a bower for the butter yellow flowers of the tall bearded Iris 'Canary Bird'. Early yellow tulips planted behind the iris have extended the colour scheme for weeks.

a useful little shrub with graceful, spreading, fan-like growth that is smothered in tiny soft pink pompon flowers on long wands. It will grow into and over small shrubs, looking particularly good over *Brachyglottis* (syn. *Senecio*) 'Sunshine' at the front of a border with a *Clematis × durandii* planted into the same hole so that its dark blue, flat flowers can contrast with the pompons.

Species roses often add that touch of grace to a bed even when most of the flowers are extremely formal. *Rosa glauca* (syn. *R. rubrifolia*) has tender grey-blue foliage with a hint of pink that produces a smoky effect – which is why you grow it. Its flowers are tiny and insignificant but pretty in their own way. If the rose is pruned to the ground in spring, it throws up the most extraordinarily exotically coloured stems that arch upwards by perhaps 2m (6–7ft) by the end of summer. Grow one behind a group of blue agapanthus and beside a swathe of *Delphinium* 'Alice Artindale', a rare double blue form.

Rosa glauca combines well with *R.* 'Ballerina' (see Fig. 11). This scheme makes a symphony of pinks, cerise, blues and purples. The roses are important elements of the design but the combination of salvias, with their furry foliage, an osteospermum, with its succulent leaves and the *Galactites tomentosa* with its narrow, white speckled leaves is a picture on its own.

All the *pimpinellifolia* roses are exquisite. They come on little scratchy bushes, but their growth is dainty and they have masses of tiny sea-green leaves. The flowers are tiny and cupped, but produced in great masses. The old 'Marbled Pink', which has white flowers whirled with pink is very pretty. The small double white, which runs and romps under birch trees where nothing else will grow, shines out at the height of summer when it is smothered in flower. 'Dunwich Rose' has single white flowers, which appear in early summer, weeping over a corner of a bed or making a neat, if prickly, edging.

For more formal borders the floribunda or cluster flowered roses cannot be beaten, although some of them are better suited to the mixed border than others. A perfect one is 'Escapade', which has all the qualities of the wild rose with single rose pink flowers with a white eye, but the strong, free-growing habits of its modern breeding. It goes with almost everything, looking beautiful with campanulas, peonies, irises and all the traditional flowers. But it looks just as good and adds a fresh touch to the flowers of autumn – *Aster × frikartii* 'Mönch', a pale blue Michaelmas daisy and *Sedum spectabile*, with its huge, flat heads of soft pink.

R. 'Rosemary Rose' makes an eye-catching combination with *R.* 'Escapade' and looks even more stunning with bright blues and the pinks of some of the best-loved herbaceous perennials. The blue-grey foliage of *Cupressus arizonicus*

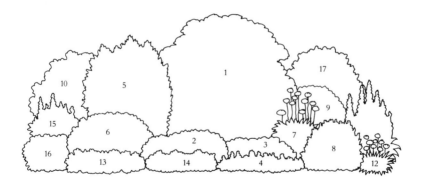

Fig. 11 *Pinks, blues and purples for a graceful late summer border.*

1 *Indigofera potaninii*
2 *Geranium × magnificum*
3 *Sedum* 'Autumn Dawn'
4 *Stachys byznatina*
5 *Rosmarinus officinalis* 'Miss Jessopp's Upright'
6 *Strobilanthes atropurpureus*
7 *Echinops ritro*
8 *Salvia sclarea* var. *turkestanica*
9 *Rosa glauca*
10 *Rosa* 'Ballerina'
11 *Acanthus spinosus*
12 *Agapanthus* 'Bressingham Blue'
13 *Galactites*
14 *Osteospermum jucundum* 'Peggyi'
15 *Penstemon* 'Apple Blossom'
16 *Erysimum* 'Bowles' Mauve'
17 *Geranium psilestemon*

var. *glabra* sets off the almost garish quality of the ephemeral blooms, and the fragile beauty of the tall- and low-growing gypsophilas acts as a brake on too much exuberance.

R. 'English Miss' has an old fashioned charm that means it mixes well with border plants, but it is a floribunda, so it flowers on and on, producing large sprays of light pink, camellia-shaped flowers with a strong, sweet scent. Planting them in groups of three throughout a long border will give the formality that suits them but will allow herbaceous perennials, like *Geranium renardii*, with its low mounds of sage green leaves and white-veined purple flowers, and blue and white campanulas, to sprawl over the ground. Add foxgloves, *Verbascum* 'Pink Domino', with its tall graceful heads of pink cups, and penstemons for later colour to give height. *Cistus* 'Silver Pink' will complement the rose, and *Stachys macrantha*, with its large furrowed soft leaves and dramatic heads of purple flower, will add another foliage element. Spear through the taller plants with drifts of lilies – white *Lilium regale* always looks and smells right and it will often naturalize. The silver filigree foliage of *Anthemis punctata* ssp. *cupaniana* will weave into such a planting, but its yellow flower heads may clash, so remove them in the bud stage. To contrast with the thread-like foliage of the anthemis, plant the substantial, smooth and rounded foliage of bergenias.

R. 'Korresia' is a cluster flowered rose that fits into mixed borders as well as it stands alone in the traditional rose garden. It is the best yellow-flowered floribunda, and the roses are particularly pretty with furled buds that open to perfect blooms. It looks good in a combination of silvers but is just as pleasing with the scarlets, oranges and yellows of crocosmia, the lime green of alchemilla, the spires of yellow and apricot kniphofias, orange tiger lilies and the massing of compact bushes of *Coreopsis verticillata* 'Zagreb', starred with bright yellow flowers in late summer. There is a more delicate version of the coreopsis, 'Moonbeam', which has a charming succession of primrose-yellow flowers for several months.

Miniature roses are becoming more and more popular, and they are increasingly used for ground cover. The ground-covering types are, however, often very rampant and difficult to contain, and they have to be cut back hard in the spring to stop the bed being dominated. The real miniatures or patio roses look best in pots, where they can be fed and watered, but the dwarf polyanthas are coming back into popularity because they are like miniature graceful shrubs. They have small, rambler-like flowers in large bunches – in fact, each bunch can be picked to make a small posy. White 'Yvonne Rabier', 'Katharina Zeimat' and 'Marie Pavié' have these qualities, and the late blooms look wonderful with the final blooms of penstemon and asters.

R. 'Nathalie Nypels' has a lot of China rose in its make-up. It has all the twiggy elegance of its forebears, but it is much tougher and seems to have a better constitution. It grows to 60cm (2ft) tall and wide and has pretty clusters of pink flowers. Buy one and make cuttings – for it roots quickly and easily on its own roots – and group it with dicentras for their feathery, bluish foliage early in the year and their pink and white flowers. Most of the dicentras look right with it, but the best is *Dicentra spectabilis*, whose lockets of pink and white hang near the rounded shapes of the rose to make a pretty picture.

'Cécile Brünner', the sweetheart rose, has exquisite blush pink flowers no larger than a thimble. They grow in flattened sprays, and if it is planted as an edger on a narrow bed in front of a deutzia, the rose will begin its season as a mound but will gradually grow up into the shrub so that its last flowers in late summer are wreathed around its branches. Some of these 'tiny' polyanthas will grow quite large if they are left unpruned and allowed to climb into other shrubs.

It is sometimes useful to have roses grown as standards to place in a bed to provide flowers above the rest of the border. A standard *R*. 'Iceberg', for example, will produce an effective display above the mass of the ordinary bushes below. 'Little White Pet' is a small shrub that spreads sideways, and it can be left unpruned to form quite a large pyramid of foliage. Tiny clusters of red buds appear in late spring, and they are followed all summer by masses of white flowers. A standard of 'Little White Pet' is striking above a sea of silver plants.

All the single simple roses blend well with shrubs and herbaceous perennials. *R*. 'White Wings' is the most glamorous, with huge papery white petals and a centre of delicious stamens that look like very long magenta eyelashes. Keep it hard pruned for the best effect.

R. 'Mrs Oakley Fisher' is a wonder in the mixed border. It is the softest apricot in colour – not a touch of harsh orange – and is one of the first hybrid teas. 'Mrs Oakley Fisher' has a graceful habit of growth and will look good in winter if unpruned, when the long stems are purpled with cold. Plant it with drifts of *Achillea* 'Taygetea', which has pale sulphur flowers that bleach to beige by autumn, and with tall aconites. The blue forms of aconite are late flowerers that bring the freshness of spring to tired late summer – the white *Aconitum* 'Ivorine' and the yellow *A. lycoctonum* ssp. *neapolitanum* flower in early summer. Unfortunately, the aconites often lose their lower leaves or turn a disgusting brown by the time the flowerheads peak, so it is as well to grow asters to disguise the unattractive lower stems. Try *Aster pringlei* 'Monte Cassino', which has delicate masses of white flowers at 1m (3ft) to just come below the massive blue heads of *Aconitum carmichaelii* 'Kelmscott', rising to almost 1.2m (4ft).

There is one rose that is not very exciting to look at, it has dull foliage and a rather lumpy shape, but I would always plant it in a bed close to my house. The people who feel roses are overplanted would never have it, but *Rosa × richardii* is the most historic of all the roses. David Austen writes: 'A rose of great historic interest, known as the Holy Rose of Abyssinia, where it has been planted from ancient times in the courtyards of Christian sanctuaries. It is said that the remains of this rose were found in the Egyptian tombs and pyramids. It is also probably the rose portrayed in the frescoes of ancient Minoan Crete.' It has flat, simple flowers, rather like those painted by primary school children, but it has all the romance in the world bred into its bones.

Overleaf: the architectural form of the silver foliage and massive flowerheads of Cynara cardunculus *(the cardoon) is a perfect foil for the tumbling masses of* Rosa *'Iceberg' in this yew-backed border.*

CHAPTER 4

TENDER AND WILD PLANTS FOR BACKGROUND COLOUR

TENDER PERENNIALS, SUBTLE ANNUALS, ornamental vegetables and self-seeding wild flowers give beds and borders a rampageous, romantic air. They fill spaces left by bulbs, bring colour to late summer plantings and always give a feeling of lushness. The self-seeders will spread over wide areas to provide a sense of continuity – one of their great virtues is their ability to flower over a long period. Some will appear in large drifts in one bed and will make only an individual appearance in a nearby border. Such flowers will look totally natural, but you will have decided which seedling should live and which should die.

Some of the more rampant self-seeders need a disciplined hand – it is all too easy to let them go and you will quickly find your best perennials overwhelmed by the luxuriant growth of valerian or forget-me-not, roses struggling through a sea of asperula and shrubs half-strangled by vinca. But they are all lovely plants that have a place in all but the tiniest gardens.

COTTAGE GARDEN FAVOURITES

Myosotis, more commonly known as forget-me-nots, wave into a blue sea in the spring garden, and they are perfect for covering the soil as they bloom for week after week. Many gardeners do not have them in their beds and borders because they can create problems. They mound up so much that they can kill precious, rare things, and they are prone to mildew. Be firm: leave enough to make a blue mist and then leave a few to seed at the back of a border when you will get more than enough to cover nearly every bed and border by the autumn. Take out all the others before they turn to black, mildewed heaps, which seems to happen overnight, when they look disgusting and will ruin your colourful borders.

The rampant self-seeder Eryngium giganteum *bears large silver thistle heads, a welcome contrast to* Lavandula angustifolia '*Hidcote*', *tall blue campanulas and* Alchemilla mollis.

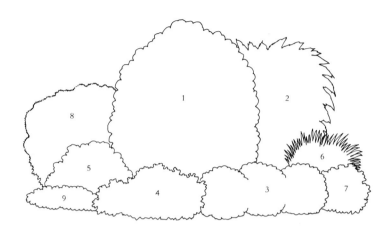

Fig. 12 *A cottage garden border using self-seeding perennials.*

1 *Cercis candensis* 'Forest Pansy'
2 *Berberis* × *ottawensis* 'Superba' and *Clematis* 'Carnaby' or *C.* 'Pink Fantasy'
3 *Rosa* 'Frensham'
4 *Salvia officinalis* Purpurascens group
5 *Foeniculum vulgare* 'Purpureum'
6 *Miscanthus sinensis* 'Undine'
7 *Monarda* 'Croftway Pink'
8 *Impatiens balsamita*
9 *Geranium robertianum*
10 *Centranthus ruber*

Centranthus ruber, or red valerian as it is called to distinguish it from the herb true valerian, is a seeder *par excellence*. In its red form it has fleshy leaves with branching heads of deep reddish-pink or white from late spring to early winter. It will drop itself into gaps in brickwork, cracks in paving and seed all over flower beds – if you let it. It has a white, woody, forked root which is difficult to get out once it is big, so beware. But there is nothing quite like it for giving an air of prodigality to a terrace bed. The beautiful white form, *C. ruber* var. *albus*, is ice cool and the star of many white gardens where it has no faults. It is easy to dead-head, and if that is done once or twice a season the plants look handsome and happy at all times.

Centranthus fits happily into wild or formal schemes (see Fig. 12). Allow it to self-seed for an informal air, but always make sure that not a single seed germinates in the root system of your roses or shrubs. In the scheme illustrated here, three self-seeders add to the air of rampant prodigality – the balsam at the back is not to be contemplated lightly, but it adds a delicate pink touch to what might otherwise be a heavyweight plan. The red and purple foliage colours of the main shrubs and roses will accentuate the flower colours of the self-seeders.

Linaria purpurea, the common toadflax, is another prolific seeder. It sends up slim stems whorled with narrowly oval, grey-green leaves topped with wands of snapdragon-like purple flowers. If snails and slugs devastate the delphiniums use this as slender substitute. It flowers for months and is quite as vivid in late summer as in spring. Some gardeners allow only *L. purpurea* 'Canon Went' into their gardens. This has bright pink flowers instead of purple ones, but it seeds just as much. A white form, *L. purpurea* 'Alba', has appeared in recent years, and it seems to build up strong colonies. It is becoming a very desirable plant, but it does not seed quite so promiscuously as the type species.

Granny's Bonnets

Granny's bonnets, the common aquilegia, with its blobby little pink flowers is rather despised by many plantspeople. But the columbine, another of its old names, is a graceful grower and is found in many more colours than muddy pink. Some are dark, almost black, and there are vivid blues, whites and spurred reds and pinks that are like flights of butterflies. There are many named forms that seed as well as *Aquilegia vulgaris*. One of the most beautiful and seeding truly, not hybridizing as so many of them do, is *A. vulgaris* 'Nora Barlow', a curious old variety with frilled, massed petals in shades of pink, white and green. The white form of *A. vulgaris* var. *stellata* has flowers just like white clematis over sea-green scalloped foliage. The foliage is one of the good points of the aquilegia – it is attractive, shaded with blue tones and when cut right back after flowering throws up new leaves that make a tidy, pretty ground cover until the first frost.

The corydalis, *Pseudofumaria lutea* (syn. *Corydalis lutea*), is an evergreen mass of finely divided, grey-green leaves. Spurred yellow flowers appear above the clumps, from spring to autumn and although it can spread with great speed around the beds and borders, its fleshy roots are easy to remove. It flits under mahonias, where its soft soapiness makes a splendid contrast to the coarser evergreen. If only the new *Corydalis flexuosa* would become such a weed.

Poppies

Welsh poppies, *Meconopsis cambrica*, in yellow and orange are forms of the highly desirable species which is regarded in some quarters as a demon weed. It can be a nuisance among small plants, but its papery petals will add a touch of glamour to sombre evergreen schemes. In sun or shade it will flower happily from spring until summer, and it is easy to tug out plants in the wrong place.

No one minds when opium poppies, *Papaver somniferum*, sow themselves around with gay abandon. Their glaucous leaves are stunning in a white border, and their hanging buds are entrancing, as long as they open white. The white doubles are the most beautiful, but even the scarlet singles have their place in mixed borders. They make wonderful seedheads which ornament early summer schemes until they turn brown and have to go. Flower arrangers love them.

White-felted leaves are always welcome, but you can have too much of them. The white, pink and magenta forms of *Lychnis coronaria* are extremely good at reproducing themselves, and tiny silver seedlings will line the bricks in a path by the end of summer if they are allowed to. They sow themselves into the heart of hellebores – and must be removed – and they make huge, spreading clumps under trees, but again they are easy to remove. The white form is particularly beautiful as a leavener with pink roses.

Polemonium caeruleum (Jacob's ladder) arouses mixed feelings. In spring its stepped, deeply divided leaves appear, to be followed in early summer by clusters of cup-shaped, lavender-blue or white flowers. In large drifts under huge shrub roses it makes a blue mist at knee height. When the flowers are over, however, it has to be carefully cut down almost at once otherwise the garden is overwhelmed with strong seedlings that can do a lot of damage to other perennials. Of its refined forms – *P.* 'Lambrook Mauve', a beautiful soft mauve, and *P. carneum*, which has silky pearl-pink flowers – you can never have too much, but they are not great seeders. *P. pauciflorum*, which has yellow flowers, seeds a little but it is never a problem. It is lovely with primroses and euphorbias.

Another dramatically good seeder is *Campanula latiloba*. It is beautiful from spring, when its slowly soaring spikes are exciting among shrubs, but once it has finished its dramatic ghostly flowering, it must be cut down at once. The spikes start to brown as soon as the first flowers have faded and the seeds are dropping and blowing before then. It makes huge woody rootstocks, and once they get into a fine peony or a group of irises it is difficult to get them out.

Brunnera macrophylla, the huge-leaved perennial that has china blue, forget-me-not-like flowers, is very handsome, but it, too, seeds prolifically and increases quickly in its large clumps. It is one of the stars of spring and makes handsome ground cover, and it would make a good companion for the campanula. In a shady corner they could compete with each, and at least the brunnera foliage would hide the unattractive finished clumps of campanula.

The comfreys have leaves that are similar to the brunnera, and they seed around the garden at great speed. The white and pure blue forms are lovely as ground cover at the backs of borders and on difficult beds where not much else will grow. They are very easy to pull or dig out, and you have the compensation of knowing that the foliage is a wonderful fertilizer. It rots down into black dust in no time, so you could leave the plants under shrubs to mulch and feed them.

Some geraniums, beautiful though they are, are such amazing seeders that they should be banned from all but the largest gardens. *Geranium* × *oxonianum* 'Claridge Druce' is a beautiful plant, with refined pink flowers, but it makes enormous clumps of overwhelming, albeit elegant, foliage that smothers anything in its way. It also seeds magnificently and will take over a large bed within a year. *Geranium procurrens* is another, although it is difficult to establish in a dry garden, in the right conditions it will romp through other plants. The cerise-purple flowers are magnificent when they are twined into *Artemisia* 'Powis Castle'.

Ordinary little violets, *Viola odorata*, which are so pretty and sweet smelling in spring, should be treated as weeds. Pull out most of them, leaving a few to entrance with their purple, mauve and white flowers.

Two more intruders – balsam and pokeweed – are very beautiful but pernicious weeds. Balsam, *Impatiens roylei* (syn. *I. glandulifera*) grows huge, fleshy stems filled with water and, unchecked, it will make 2m (6–7ft) in two or three months. The sweetly scented flowers are pouched like orchids, and people who see it always want it until they see how much of it there is. Although it is easy to pull out in early spring, there is always so much else to do then, that the innocuous little seedlings are left for another day, and then it is very difficult to get out because it makes an overground root system that anchors it firmly.

Pokeweed, *Phytolacca* ssp., has two variants, the Chinese and the American. Both are shocking pink, beautiful and shockingly difficult to get rid of, but there is nothing quite like them in late summer. They have very ordinary foliage but lovely pink pokers, packed with starry flowers that change gradually into the most delicious looking black-stained red berries. The roots and berries are poisonous, and pokeweed should never be planted where children might be tempted. Birds love them, however, and carry the seeds all over the garden. In the United States it is believed that the roots of the Virginia pokeweed, *Phytolacca americana*, sterilize the ground, making it impossible to grow anything else. The roots are on a massive scale and must take immense amounts of nutrients out of the soil. The Chinese species, *P. clavigera*, has bright crimson stems, which make it even more attractive. Keep this monster plant at the back of flower borders, where its leaves are hidden and only the stems and flowers show above a group of *Rosa mundi*, out of flower by late summer and happy to have the pokers pushing through its foliage. Drape a late-flowering clematis, such as *C. 'Jackmanii'*, to bloom in purple splendour over the rose foliage to harmonize with the pink pokers.

An entirely different self-seeder is the evening primrose, *Oenothera biennis*, which grows to 0.9–1.2m (3–4ft) in a season and reveals its pale yellow flowers, one by one. Miraculously, they seem to open at about four o'clock in the afternoon – one minute you have a tall, leafy stem hung with buds heavy with promise and then a petal suddenly extends, it shimmers alone for a minute and then more and more petals are unfurled until the stem is a miracle of primroses. By evening the scent is heady. They seed themselves gently around and it is always pleasing to find next year's seedlings looking like flattened stars in different parts in the garden. In fact, there are never quite enough.

Sweet cicely, *Myrrhis odorata*, is a beautiful ferny plant of the freshest green in spring. It goes well with the evening primrose, whose later flowers will be supported by the strong growth of the cicely. White umbels of flower crowd the stems early in the year to make one of the most lovely spring sights, but cut it down at once, otherwise there will be a monster regiment of little ferny plants seeded into the roses or the euphorbias. Some seedlings always escape, so you will never be without it.

It is possible to make a garden of these self-seeding plants. As long as the gardener remains in control it is a cheap and beautiful way of clothing the soil. It would, for instance, be possible to let the above plants seed happily together and add in one *Verbascum olympicum*, one of the best of the seeding verbascums. This is a biennial, like the evening primrose, and provides an even more impressive vertical, with its silky white, furry leaves and stems rising above 1.8m (6ft). It has magnificent branching candelabra of yellow blossoms in midsummer, sometimes into autumn, if the mullein moth does not get them first.

Onopordum acanthium is a gigantic thistle, whose whiteness matches the verbascum. It is the most dramatic feature plant and looks perfect surrounded by a sea of silvers. Because it is exceptionally spiny and stiff, it stands out like a silver skeleton against a dark background. In late summer it has pale lilac thistle flowers and then it dies, leaving a legacy of solitary seedlings that appear in the strangest places the following year.

Fennel, *Foeniculum vulgare*, is similar. In its bronze or green form it soars to 2.7m (9ft) in the summer, with lime green flower heads over filmy, insubstantial foliage. Use the leaves and seeds in cooking, and thin out most of the seedlings, which can become a nuisance.

Both decorative and useful, feathery fennel, Foeniculum vulgare, *grows in a mixed border of yellow flowers and foliage.* Lonicera nitida *'Baggesen's Gold' is clipped into a dome to accentuate the flowing form of* Sedum acre var. aurem *at its feet and the masses of white snakeroot,* Eupatorium rugosum, *and yellow lupins.*

Spendthrift Seeders

Annuals like love-in-a-mist, *Nigella damascena*, and cornflowers, *Centaurea cyanus*, need be sown only once. For ever afterwards you will get crowds of seedlings, and because they are so numerous they can do a lot of damage to finer plants. Nevertheless, a host of foaming blueness from the *Nigella's* many petalled and spurred flowers appearing over feathery bright green foliage to contrast with the flat, solid stars of the cornflower – is very attractive, especially when it is highlighted by a group of self-seeded scarlet opium poppies. They are all spendthrift seeders and have to be carefully controlled, without letting the discipline show.

Little pansies join in this mêlée very happily. Most pansies and violas will revert to type as they seed, but they are very attractive and will find their way into shrubs and roses to flower at quite a height.

When is a Weed not a Weed?

Some people are surprised to see feverfew, *Tanacetum parthenium*, growing in a cultivated garden. It is exceptionally prolific as a seeder, but the foliage of the yellow-foliaged form, *T. parthenium* 'Aureum', is astonishingly bright early in the year, and it makes an excellent edging for paths. The green form, which has double white button flowers, is good in shade and will seed itself happily into hedge bottoms. The divided foliage is powerfully scented and will overwhelm small, finer plants if it is allowed to.

Herb Robert, *Geranium robertianum*, is entrancing in the late winter. Its fern-like leaves appear over red shoots, and it fills in the most unlikely places with its pretty foliage. Pink flowers come and go all spring and summer, then the plant turns dark red and goes. Encourage it under trees where nothing else will grow.

Honesty, *Lunaria annua*, especially in its beautifully variegated form, is also a lovely sight under trees. The mauve form, which has plain green leaves, is not to be despised, for it makes a cloud of colour under birches early in spring to go with narcissus and tulips. The white flowers of the variegated form, *L. annua* 'Alba Variegata', look magnificent banked under acers and at the foot of roses.

Even hellebores, the least weedy of plants and the sophisticated gardener's favourite plant, will self-seed around with great abandon. The experts say that most of the self-sown plants will have muddy pink flowers, but sometimes a brilliantly spotted one occurs, and if you keep your varieties separately – all the white ones in a bed on their own, if possible – they seem to come true. Most of them are so beautiful with handsome evergreen foliage that all are welcome, however.

DECORATIVE AND EDIBLE

Many modern gardens are far too small to have a separate vegetable or herb garden, but it is easy to incorporate the plants into the flower beds. Some herbs are highly ornamental in their own right; most have aromatic leaves and interesting flowers. The plain ones – coriander, flat-leaved parsley, dill and tarragon, for example – can be grown in pots by the back door.

We have already noted that many decorative herbs, including curled parsley, sage in all its many coloured forms – silver, purple and yellow – thyme, chives and majoram, are as good as foliage and flowering plants as any perennial. However, there are at least six vegetables that are just as ornamental. All will give lots of produce and make architectural elements in a border.

First, the artichokes, two of which have the most handsome foliage of any herbaceous plant. The cardoon, *Cynara cardunculus*, is huge and silver; you can eat the leaf stems if you can ever bear to pick them. Its less dramatic sister, the globe artichoke, *C. scolymus*, has softer, smaller leaves, but is just as telling in a smaller border. Its heads are picked and eaten before they open to massive purple thistles. Grow several, eat some and admire the rest.

Next, is the Jerusalem artichoke, *Helianthus tuberosus*. This is not an artichoke at all, and it has nothing to do with Israel, but is native to North America. It is a member of the sunflower family and makes an enormously tall plant with soft hairy leaves topped with huge sunflowers. It looks good at the back of a flower bed and can be eaten in early winter when the knobbly tubers are dug and cooked at once. The name Jerusalem comes from the French, who called the plants 'girasol', when they were first imported from the New World in 1605 because they turned their flower faces to the sun. It was the English who corrupted the name.

Jane Grigson, one of the great cookery writers, said of the artichoke and asparagus: 'the artichoke was the aristocrat of the Renaissance kitchen garden as the asparagus was of the Roman. It is sobering to realize they are still the two finest vegetables we can grow.'

Asparagus is traditionally grown in raised, segregated beds, but I find it does just as well in a flower border. Even if it is kept in a proper bed, the self-sown seedlings find their way into well-manured beds to produce excellent spears. Asparagus fern, which foams upwards after cutting time is over, makes a fine foil for dark shrubs.

French beans, *Phaeseolus vulgaris*, the scarlet runners, were introduced to Europe from America by John Tradescant, gardener to King Charles I, as a flowering plant. The flowers were used in posies and for decorating houses, but today we grow it in the vegetable garden in trenches and up bamboo poles and eat the beans constantly in summer. If those same poles are tied together as a wigwam and put as a centrepiece or a corner incident in beds or borders, the bean flowers are just as elegant as they were 250 years ago. Today, we have varieties with white, pink or red flowers, and the beans can be purple as well as green, making it a plant for all seasons.

Cabbages and leeks are the prosaic stuff of winter meals, but they are magnificent border plants. A few leek plants, *Allium porrum*, dibbed in to a bed in late spring will grow huge, luscious swathes of foliage and produce massive seed heads if you do not pick them. Those rounded balls of white are as impressive as the most expensive ornamental *Allium*, to which they are, after all, closely related. Most cabbages are fit only for the vegetable garden, but the varieties with smaller, pewter-grey leaves are excellent as edgers and only have to be cut when winter is imminent and most border plants have already retreated below ground. There are now many strains of ornamental cabbage with pink and white foliage. The peacock strain is even better: it has frilled and jagged edges to the outer colourful leaves and a magnificently striped heart. They make good winter pot plants as well.

Salad plants, little onions and lettuce in all their many coloured and differently leaved forms, are pretty edging plants, which can be planted over early spring bulbs and in place of winter bedding. They will not flower unless you let them go to seed, but at the height of summer there should be enough colour in the flower bed behind. Buy a packet of seed labelled 'Salad Bowl' and you will be able to cut and come again for a selection of red, bronzed and green leaves all summer and have a border edge at the same time.

Atriplex hortensis var. *rubra* is called New Zealand spinach or purple orach, and its cardinal red leaf tips are pretty in a salad and handsome in the border. In spring there is a forest of little pink seedlings, which gradually extend into 1.8m (6ft) giants. They are always stunningly red in stem, leaf and flower. When they run to seed they do so in enormous sheaves of pink discs, and the whole plant shimmers and shines in sunlight. It seeds happily. Ruby chard is as good with its beetroot red stems and shining, green leaves that take a colour wash from their midribs. Both stems and leaves are eaten – separately and at different times – so it is a two-for-the-price-of-one vegetable. It, too, goes to seed wondrously, and it is worth keeping as an ornamental rather than as a culinary plant.

The same can be said for seakale, *Crambe maritima*, whose leaf midribs can be steamed and eaten when they have been blanched. It makes an even more impressive border plant in a hot, dry place, when immense, flat, grey leaves will spread out over the surface while new growth crimps up in the centre of the plant. Eventually it bears huge panicles of white blossom. You will not get the flowers if you eat it.

In its cultivated form, *Cichorium intybus* is known as chicory, endive or batavia. A packet of seed will produce a row of tight little red and green balls, rather like a Webb's Wonder lettuce only smoother and harder. Good cooks blanch the shoots in a dark cupboard, but you can eat some of the leaves and even cook one or two whole hearts that have been decorating the flower beds. The ones left to seed produce gigantic flower heads of china blue daisies to provide self-sown seedlings, which will appear in the paths and beds. They are easily moved.

Have fun with your gardening and make a small vegetable patch in a bed or border with vegetables (see Fig. 13). The leaf colours are a mixture of grey, sea greens and dusky purples to make a garden picture in themselves.

UPPER-CRUST ANNUALS

Annuals, the flowers whose seed has to be sown every year to get a display for the whole summer, are the flowers that go on week after week. Beds of huge French marigolds, scarlet salvias and the dot-and-carry effect of white alyssum and blue lobelia are not, however, a form of gardening that really fits with herbaceous perennials and shrub roses.

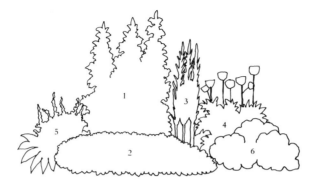

Fig. 13 *An ornamental vegetable patch for late summer and early autumn colour.*

1 *Atriplex hortensis*   4 Artichoke
2 *Crambe maritima*   5 Chicory
3 Asparagus   6 Ornamental cabbage

It is, however, possible to use traditional bedding plants in herbaceous beds and borders to great effect. Swathes of white alyssum at the front of a border, sweeping back into masses of roses, banks of blue lobelia trailing into a planting of silver stachys and lychnis are interesting ways to use these traditional plants. Of more use in the mixed border are the subtle, elegant annuals – nicotianas, cosmos and lavateras, phacelias, antirrhinums, limnanthes and sweet peas.

Tobacco plants, *Nicotiana* ssp., are seen in almost all the best gardens these days. Look out for refined forms – *N. alata* (syn. *N. affinis*) 'Lime Green' and *N. langsdorfii*, which are both in shades of green and brown. White *N. alata* is the best for scent, for nowadays few of the others smell at all. The Sensation Series comes in bright colours of pink and red and should be fragrant. There is a new 'Domino Pink', with pale salmon flowers that look beautiful with silvered euonymus and blue agapanthus. Many plants overwinter to build up into huge clumps by next summer.

Nicotiana sylvestris, flowering tobacco, is the annual *par excellence* for woodland gardens. It easily reaches 1.5m (5ft), has huge basal leaves and immense great candelabra of white, long-tubed flowers. It is exciting at the back of any border. Save the seeds because even though it usually overwinters, it seems to take ages to come into flower and often only by early autumn if you rely on your old ones. Sow seed of all nicotianas in late winter, in a warm greenhouse, and grow them on in separate pots for massive summer flowering plants ready to put out at the beginning of summer.

Cosmos are slight, feathery annuals at the beginning of their lives, but if they are not starved and planted too closely, they grow to almost shrub-like

Nicotiana langsdorffii *bears its graceful green bells in a late summer grouping of dark red sedum and silver* Artemisia stelleriana. *The blue starry flowers of* Linum narbonense *and the fluffy masses of pale* Stipa tenuissima *add colour and contrast.*

proportions, massed with delicate but large daisies in red, deep pink and a sensational white. They are a lovely accompaniment for old roses and will weave into the once-flowered shrub to give it a second life.

Lavatera trimestris 'Silver Cup' is laden with rose pink flowers. When it reaches its zenith it can be almost 1m (3ft) wide and completely smothered by large, trumpet-shaped flowers as much as 10cm (4in) across. The white cultivar, *L. trimestris* 'Mont Blanc', has glistening, pure white flowers but is smaller and much more delicate.

Annual edgers are often much more floriferous than a small herbaceous perennial, and a particularly good one is *Phacelia campanularia*, the California bluebell. The intense blue of its thimble flowers is almost comparable to the blue gentians. *Echium* 'Blue Bedder' has china blue flowers and blooms for a long time on a sunny edge. It looks especially striking with drifts of white nicotiana and stands of Brugmansia, one of the great summer exotics.

For a change of colour and just as easy an edger is the poached egg plant, *Limnathes douglasii*, also known as meadow foam in California where it is indigenous. It is one of the most free-flowering annuals in cultivation, with its mossy foliage which is literally covered with yellow-centred white flowers for weeks. It often flowers itself to death, but seedlings soon appear all around and it is off again.

Antirrhinums, *Antirrhinum* ssp., and sweet peas, *Lathyrus odoratus*, are other easy annuals to join seamlessly into a mixed border as well as being delights on their own or in a bedding scheme. Antirrhinums come in most colours, except blue, and sweet peas have blue, purple and mauve to extend the range. All the ornamental peas can be grown up tripods, especially the decorative obelisks, towers and metal fountains that can now be bought. The antirrhinum is good for massing in drifts of separate colours throughout beds and borders that are tired after a busy spring. One of the most beautiful varieties is *Antirrhinum majus* 'Taff's Double', which has clean cream and green variegated foliage and clear white flowers.

TENDER PERENNIALS

The aristocrats of the bedding world are the great tender perennials and exotics from tropical countries. This last category includes plants like *Brugmansia* (syn. *Datura*), *Ricinus communis*, cannas, the coloured phormiums and banana plants, all of which have huge, magnificent leaves and exciting flowers. The colours are not to everyone's taste. They are in vibrant shades of orange, scarlet and bronze, which can look harsh under insipid skies, although they are thrilling in the sun. They are definitely not to be mixed with old shrub roses.

Most of these plants have to be wintered indoors, especially in Britain, except honeybush, *Melianthus major*, which will become established in time in sheltered gardens. It is a South African species, which provides a strikingly sub-tropical effect in all-white gardens. It has glaucous, deeply-toothed, long leaves and tubular flowers in tawny crimson. If you dare not risk it outside, lift it from the border in late autumn or grow it in a pot and sink it into the ground for the summer months. You can do this with most tropical plants, but the cordyline, the popular leafy plant that showers out like a firework in greens and reds, must always be left in its pot – it hates root disturbance. Gertrude Jekyll frequently used this trick to keep borders going, and the exotic plants do put a bit of zing into a flagging planting. A blue-leaved or white and yellow striped agave, in an important pot, is excellent for spicing up a planting of evergreens.

If you like the idea of exotic bedding you will have to provide either greenhouse or conservatory space for them. Most of them look just as good in winter as summer, so you will have the benefit twice over. They will even live quite happily in spare bedrooms and most of them can be cut hard back or pruned down to take less space. The banana, *Musa basjoo*, or one of its relatives is one of these. All its leaves can be stripped away in late autumn so that just the stem is left for easy storage. Some gardeners plant them out into borders, where they find many smaller runners from them at the end of summer to make new plants. Of course, they will not fruit in cool temperate climates unless under glass, and even then only rarely. However, in a sheltered bed they will provide a dramatic accent, and even in windy beds they still make exciting verticals.

Ricinus communis, the castor-oil plant, in its many variations may have striking bronze-red, huge green palmate or dark purple foliage. It grows speedily and easily from seed and sometimes has little pompons of flower. It looks magnificent

The scarlet flowers of Dahlia '*Bishop of Llandaff*' *gleam in the late summer border. The hot colour is tempered by a group of tall pinkish-purple* Eupatorium purpureum *and drifts of silver* Brachyglottis, *grasses and a variegated euphorbia.*

with cannas. *Canna* × *generalis* hybrids are available from specialist bulb growers in spring. They have flamboyant yellow, scarlet or orange flowers and strange angled seedheads. The cultivar 'Wyoming' has magnificent dark red leaves with orange flowers, and it makes a vibrant pairing with *Dahlia* 'Bishop of Llandaff', with its scarlet and maroon colour scheme in a shockingly exciting way. Cannas can, in fact, be treated just like dahlias. They should be cut down once the frost comes and kept dry over winter in a frost-free place. If you have a small patio or terrace bed where there are no pinks, whites or pale blues, these exotic plants will bring a clash of colour like nothing else in your garden. But keep them well away from anything subtle or quietly beautiful.

Phormiums in their plain or coloured forms have dramatic sword-like foliage that is almost a dangerous. All the leaves have sharp points. The green *Phormium tenax* is hardy in some areas, but it is not a mixer. It makes an excellent accent in the border, but when its flowers soar to 3m (10ft) with great bronzed flights of orange, bird-like flowers, it is best with the other exotics in a hot place.

Brugmansia suaveolens is the most beautiful of all the flowering exotics. Also called daturas, they are the angels' trumpets of South America. They will grow into a 1.8m (6ft) tall woody shrub in one season and will carry as many as twenty-four huge white bells of flower at once. The scent is sensational and is supposed to be so heady that it will overwhelm you. They are most beautiful in their white forms, although the pink is nearly as pretty. They can be planted out once frosts are over and they will grow from cuttings taken in late summer. You could keep one in a pot and tuck it into a bed around a terrace so that you can simply move it indoors in winter. They are gross feeders and should be given tomato fertilizer every day if possible. In autumn cut it right back, take it indoors and put it by a north-facing window until the new leaves grow.

Datura inoxia has large flawless flowers up to 20cm (8in) long in the palest shade of lilac. One flower will scent a whole greenhouse and is quite unforgettable. It is a half-hardy annual and may be grown every year from seed.

Diascias, verbenas, petunias and argyranthemums are all good bedding subjects. They are easily raised from cuttings and can be planted out *en masse* in beds where earlier flowers have faded.

Diascia rigescens is superb in pink and grey plantings. It will follow peonies and climb through silver *Artemesia ludoviciana* to flower all summer, as long as it is dead-headed. *D.* 'Salmon Supreme' does not even need dead-heading – it goes on flowering all summer with its tiny salmon flowers forming a perfect contrast in a hot border with drifts of blue or white agapanthus flowers dangling overall.

Verbenas are weavers and will move into a flower bed to drape perennials and shrubs with continuous umbels of flower. *V.* 'Sissinghurst' is cerise pink, *V.* 'Hidcote Purple' is blue, and there is a scarlet version that is magnificent with oranges and red to create a vibrant clashing mixture. Best of all is *V.* 'Silver Anne', which is pink overlaid with misty gauze. In the right place it will stay from year to year.

Petunias are usually raised from seed and come in white, yellow, pink, red, purple and blue. The Big Daddy types are shadowed with grey, and the Picotee ones are frilled and bi-coloured. The Japanese have bred a new petunia that is an enormous grower. Just one in a bed will swamp smaller treasures, and it is best planted with big shrubs, even growing up and into the bare legs of the biggest roses. Known as Surfina petunias, they are grown from cuttings, not from seed, and the white one with blue veins is a marvel.

MARGUERITES BY ANY OTHER NAME

Marguerites, the staple of summer pot plants, are as good in the border. They grow quickly and easily from cuttings, even when they are just tucked into soil where they are needed. The genus name has been changed to *Argyranthemum*, from *Chrysanthemum*, but they are still as useful for bedding as before. *Argyranthemum* will be scorched but not killed by light frost, so it can be hardened off in spring and planted out in early summer fairly safely. It will make big plants by midsummer.

Argyranthemum 'Jamaica Primrose' is one of the best bedders. It makes sturdy, 60cm (2ft) high shrubs, spangled all over with yellow daisies. It needs dead-heading at least twice in a season to keep it flowering and looking smart, although people with time on their hands can do it every week. It is an excellent plant to replace early wallflowers where you need the same sort of effect. One of the finest in style as well as texture is *A. gracile* 'Chelsea Girl', which has finely cut, almost hair-like silver foliage and single white flowers. It contrasts well with all the smooth and furry leaved silvers but is beautiful, too, with floribunda pink roses. *A.* 'Apricot Surprise' is a soft orange, excellent with yellow grasses, helianthemums, *Lilium* 'African Queen' with its tawny trumpets, and a tall plant of an abutilon with apricot flowers and variegated leaves.

Argyranthemum 'Mary Wootton' is a soft, pretty pink with double flowers, sugary sweet with fondant pink petunias, *Rosa* 'English Miss' and spires of pink verbascums. *A. maderense* is a species with blue-grey leaves, starred with primrose yellow tiny daisies on a neat shrub. The list of varieties named every year is getting rather long, but best of the rest are *A.* 'Blizzard', with shaggy double white flowers, *A.* 'Vancouver', which is deeper pink double flowers, and *A.* 'Sark' a pure white double. There is also a delightful tiny single pink that is lovely, and the muddy *A.* 'Rollason's Red', which is disappointing.

Abutilons are tallish shrubs that may live for quite a time in a sheltered border. They are easily propagated from seed or by cuttings in summer, but they are just the plants for a double life, their pots sunk into a border for the summer and their bells enchanting in a conservatory in the winter. *Abutilon* 'Canary Bird' has beautiful butter-yellow flowers, which hang in fat sheened pouches from boughs decorated with dark vine-shaped leaves. It is lovely over the miniature bamboo *Pleioblastus viridistriatus*, which is not rampant and which has satin smooth yellow leaves striped with green. Add an apricot argyranthemum and *Helichrysum petiolare*, a tender grey shrub that will weave around them all. The helichrysum is well known as a pot plant, but it is even better in a bed where it will grow rampantly and flower profusely. Sometimes it will get through the winter to make an even bigger plant next year.

Abutilon 'Canary Bird' grows to a neat 1.2m (4ft), but *A.* 'Ashford Red' will achieve the proportions of a small tree in a season. Cut back the branches to make it more compact. It has evergreen, maple-shaped leaves, which set off the bell-shaped crimson flowers that are borne nearly all the year. With the red abutilon try growing a *Rhodochiton atrosanguineum*, a tender climber, which has unusual, tubular blackish-purple flowers with bell-shaped, reddish-purple calyces

Tender pot plants, like marguerites, make lovely border subjects. Argyranthemum *'Jamaica Primrose' mingles with* A. *'Peach Cheeks' and* Nicotiana langsdorffii.

for at least six months. It will scramble up into the branches of the abutilon to hang decoratively along their lengths, contrasting and complementing the abutilon flowers. This abutilon is easy to grow from cuttings taken in spring, but the rhodochiton is best grown fresh each year from seed.

There is always scope for experiment with bedding and as it is so ephemereal it is fun to choose exciting new flowers every year.

CHAPTER 5

ELEGAIC AUTUMN

THE GARDEN SLOWLY TURNS as the days get shorter, and foliage colours veer wildly from bonfire reds and yellows to the fading primroses and beige of failing hosta leaves. Scarlet and gold flowers predominate, but the skilful use of late-flowering plants can bring all the freshness of spring back into the border. The great bells of Brugmansia, for example, the tiered steeples of *Nicotiana sylvestris* and the endless scented flowers of evening primrose will help to keep the borders intoxicating.

Nevertheless, summer's transition into autumn does rely heavily on the tawny shades, with buff ornamental grasses and crimson, brown and black seedheads accentuating the yellow-green foliage. The end of summer goes in a flash of yellow as all the members of the daisy family have been at their best. The most welcome flowers now will be those that bloom for the first time, not on their second flush.

COOL BLUE

In the first misty, damp days of autumn a haze of blue flowers goes with the elegaic air and is a foil for the yellowness all around. Add plenty of silvers, which look good up until hard frosts, and even then some will shine on into the winter.

Start with the shrub layer, to fan out under a small tree, a *Koelreuteria paniculata*, the golden rain tree, which in early autumn bears enormous panicles of yellow flowers. The big seedheads follow later and are nearly as decorative. Ceratostigma, a graceful shrub with healthy dark green leaves, is laden with tiny blue flowers – just like those of plumbago – right through early autumn. *C. griffithii* is a beautiful Himalayan species with very deep blue flowers; *C. willmottianum* has rich blue flowers combined with foliage that turns a brilliant red by late autumn. *C. griffithii* is more shrub like than *C. willmottianum*, which is often almost herbaceous, and it should be cut down to the ground in spring to produce a dome-shaped shrub rather than a great sprawling mass. It also flowers much better if pruned.

Caryopteris is a most graceful shrub. It has arching grey leaved branches, which should be hard pruned in spring, starred all over with intense blue flowers. A group planted on the corner of a bed will be an eye-catching feature. It is easy to grow from cuttings taken when you prune the bush. There are some exceptionally good named forms of the plant. Look out for *C.* 'Heavenly Blue' or 'Ferndown', but try to see them in flower in a garden centre before you buy so that you choose the best. Caryopteris likes to be in full sun, so plant two or three to the side of the tree where the blueness will be exhilarating.

To contrast with the tiny leaves of the shrub, plant *Strobilanthes atropurpureus*, an unusual perennial that throws up jointed, woody stems rather like a shrub. The oval yet pointed leaves, are covered with fine silvery hairs, and the ink blue flowers are held high above the 1m (3ft) growth. Even taller and throwing a blue veil across this planting would be drifts of *Echinops ritro*, which have rounded, soft heads that look as if they ought to be prickly. You need buy only one because they are promiscuous self-seeders and you will soon have a forest.

The brightest blue of any autumn flower is found on *Salvia patens*, but the plants have to be treated like dahlias and taken up, or cuttings taken regularly. It grows readily from seed, and there is nothing quite like its intense gentian blue. An easier salvia for autumn is *S. uliginosa*. Terrifically tall, up to 1.8m (6ft) in the right conditions, it will thread its porcelain blue flowers in and out of a blue scheme quite happily, increasing year by year as long as you cover the roots with mulch for protection in winter.

Spires and spikes contrast best with these mostly rounded shapes, and *Perovskia atriplicifolia* fits the bill admirably. It is one of the most beautiful small subshrubs and associates well with so many things, particularly other blue flowers, silvers like lavender and, in an irresistible combination, *Sedum spectabile*. The sedum has flat heads of palest pink, while *S.* 'Autumn Joy' has deep rich pink flowers. This is a striking plant from the moment its sea green-coloured buds appear in late winter to when its flower heads fade to tan.

The perovskia and sedum team well with autumn-flowering asters. Some people cannot bear Michaelmas daisies, probably because they associate them with the mildew to which some of the older varieties of the *novi-belgii* cultivars were prone. In the last few years many new ones have been introduced and they are magnificent. *Aster thomsonii* 'Nanus', a superb daisy with clear light blue flowers, is perfect with sedum.

ASTERS

Aster divaricatus is not new, but it looks exquisite over the dark, thick leaves of bergenia, which show its shiny black stems and sprays of white daisies to great effect. The aster often falls forwards over the bergenia, looking like a cloud of tiny butterflies that are taking a rest. With the same sort of flowers, but arching upwards into great puffs of fluffy white blooms, is *Aster tradescantii*. Its feathery foliage looks lovely when combined with groups of grasses, which are at their best in autumn. *A. pringlei* 'Monte Cassino' and *A. ericoides* 'Pink Cloud' are two of the newer asters that produce great cumulus clouds of bloom to lighten the heaviness of fading borders.

In a class of its own is *Aster lateriflorus* 'Horizontalis', a strongly structured plant that achieves shrub-like proportions by early autumn – compact and wide – with minute white flowers with fluffy pink-purple centres massed all over the plant.

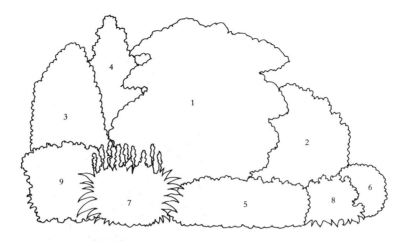

Fig. 14 *Fiery colours for the autumn, enhanced by underplanting* Colchicum autumnale *and*
Crocus speciosus.

1 *Acer palmatum* 'Senkaki'
2 *Viburnum tinus*
3 *Garrya elliptica*
4 *Chamaecyparis lawsoniana* 'Lanei'
5 *Aster lateriflorus* 'Horizontalis'

6 *Aster pringlei* 'Monte Cassino'
7 *Iris foetidissima* var. *citrina*
8 *Sedum spurium* 'Atropurpureum'
9 *Dendranthema* 'Bronze Elegance'

It is spectacular grown as a small hedge or as a tallish edging for a long bed, and
its outline remains all winter to be cut down to ground level in early spring,
when tiny bulbs planted underneath come through to take its place. It looks
good planted in a mixed border where its subtle colour scheme will be an anchor
in a brilliant display of reds and purples (see Fig. 14). Its purple flush is
accentuated by the darkness of *Sedum spurium* 'Atropureum', matched by the
flowers of the *Viburnum tinus* and enriched by the brilliant scarlet of the bark of
Acer palmatum 'Senkaki'. The bonfire effect is enhanced by the coppery tones of
Dendranthema 'Bronze Elegance' and the golden glow of a conifer.

Two other asters are indispensable for wonderful splashes of colour in mid-
autumn. *A. novae-angliae* 'Harrington's Pink' has satiny soft pink flowers that are
quite large but appear in huge numbers all over a tall plant. *A. novae-angliae*
'Alma Potschke' has spectacular sheets of astonishingly vivid cherry-red flowers.
If you have a large garden a massed planting of all different heights and types of
aster makes an amazing impression

DAHLIAS AND CHRYSANTHEMUMS

The large and colourful chrysanthemums and dahlias are, in my view, best kept
for the cutting beds that are often part of a vegetable garden. The smaller daisy-
like dahlias, however, are good border subjects. *D.* 'Preference' has pretty pink
cactus flowers and reasonable foliage, and it mixes well with the aconites which
go on flowering with purple spikes well into autumn.

D. 'Bishop of Llandaff' is completely different. At its best in autumn, it looks wonderful in a bed of purple foliage with hot-coloured flowers. The leaves are darkest plum, with a tremendous gleam, which set off the satiny scarlet petals and yellow stamens. It is a big grower, not really suitable for a small bed. You could grow it in a container, but like other dahlias it must be lifted, cut back and stored in winter, with most of the earth shaken off the tubers, which must be stored in a dry, frost-free shed or garage. In spring, when the tubers start into life again, the tubers can be returned to the container.

The old, hardy chrysanthemums are always welcome. The genus name has been changed to *Dendranthema*, but the flowers are as good as ever. *D.* 'Bronze Elegance' is a must for the garden where there are a lot of hot colours, and its long-lasting, gold-bronzed flowers are magnificent against a planting of *Symphytum* × *uplandicum* 'Variegatum' so that the comfrey gracefully disguises the rather bare lower stems of the *Dendranthema*. The large-leaved comfrey has the cleanest cream variegation of any herbaceous plant. Stunning with the *Symphytum* and a few late *Anemone* × *hybrida* is *Dendranthema* 'Emperor of China'. This has amazing burgundy-coloured leaves in autumn that set off the deep pink flowers, fading to silver just like a self-contained flower arrangement.

Several good autumn flowers are pink. *Nerine bowdenii* suddenly appears through the ground with its amazingly bright cerise pink flowers. They look rather exotic, as if they would be most at home in a greenhouse, but, planted correctly, they are quite hardy. They like a hot, dry bed close to a south-facing wall so that their bulbs ripen. Do not plant them too deeply, or they will not flower. They look very beautiful next to a planting of slate blue *Scutellaria scordiifolia*, which has hooded, lipped flowers. It likes heat and, like the nerine, needs a little shelter.

Origanums are good in hot spots and contrast with the shocking pink of the nerine. *O. laevigatum* 'Herrenhausen', is, as yet, little known, but it is proving to be an excellent small herbaceous perennial. The violet flowers edged in dark maroon start to appear in late summer, and the stems elongate until they spray out across a path.

Two members of the blackberry family are stars of autumn. *Rubus phoenicolasius*, the Japanese wineberry, reaches its peak then, with huge pink bristly stems, vine-shaped leaves, white felted underneath, and clusters of bright coral pink berries. The birds leave them until late autumn, almost winter, but humans often find them irresistible before then. If Japanese wineberry is handsome, *R. ulmifolius* 'Bellidiflorus' is pretty. It has the same sort of stems and leaves as the wineberry but no berries. Instead it has large panicles of double pink flowers, just like tiny powder puffs. It is extremely vigorous and must be chopped back every spring, but it is containable at the back of a big border.

To accompany the *Rubus*, grow one of the spindle family. *Euonymus alatus*, which has flattened, corky stems, has the most brilliant autumn colour, but *E.*

Two stars of the autumn garden – Dendranthema *'White Gloss' and the bright pink* Anemone × hybrida *'Prinz Heinrich' – add a touch of glamour to the border.*

The dark green leaves of the winged spindle, Euonymus alatus, *turn a wonderful brilliant scarlet colour in autumn.*

europaeus 'Red Cascade' has the most striking fruit dangling in long red showers. *E. planipes* (syn. *E. sachalinensis*) has magnificent autumn colour and strange, lobed red fruit dangling on long pedicels that burst open to reveal orange seeds. *E. latifolius* has lax stems with leaves that turn from green to rose red to claret. The bright pink fruits are like little square boxes, which spring open to reveal their seeds.

Many trees and shrubs colour wonderfully in autumn, but most of the large ones are better in a woodland setting. From late summer *Malus* 'Golden Hornet' is covered in gorgeous yellow crabapples, while *M.* 'John Downie' has rose-flushed cream fruits. Both trees will grow to 10m (30ft).

Sorbus is a large genus, containing many species that have brilliant autumn colours in their tiny chandeliers of berries. The species bearing orange and red fruits are commonly seen, but the white- and pink-berried forms are small, delicate trees that are excellent in island beds or large borders. *S. cashmiriana* has fruits like white china beads, which droop for months after the leaves have fallen; *S. hupehensis* has blue-green leaves, which turn crimson in autumn just as the white berries are turning to pink; *S. vilmorinii* has fern-like leaves, which turn red and purple late in the year, and hanging rose-red fruits, which turn through pink to white.

Prettier than flowers and strikingly effective, are the pink leaves and chalk white berries of Sorbus cashmiriana, *seen here growing through an underplanting of yellow-edged* Daphne odora *'Aureomarginata'.*

Colchicums grow from corms, and they can be spring- or autumn-flowering. They are the 'naked ladies' of history, so named because the flower stems rise up smooth and unadorned by leaves. The Ancient Egyptians used an extract of the plants as a remedy against gout, and it is still so used. *Colchicum speciosum*, which has large pink to purple flowers in autumn, is difficult to place in the mixed border because the large leaves come in vast quantities in spring and die down unattractively just as the great flowering season gets into swing. The answer is to plant the corms just behind a low-growing herbaceous perennial, such as a hardy geranium, which will come into leaf to hide the dying leaves and be finished by the time the colchicums come into flower.

Cyclamens are always beautiful and are easy to grow from corms. They are smothered with little pink or purplish flags of flowers from late summer into autumn. *C. hederifolium* is the autumn-flowering species; *C. coum* flowers from winter to early spring. They grow happily in the shade of trees, forming huge, round corms. The corms sometimes mound up against each other, but it is best to move them before they get to that state. Once you have built up a colony you will find plenty of self-sown seedlings around, sometimes in the most inappropriate places like the lawn. Dig them up carefully in spring, just before

The autumn-flowering crocus, Colchicum autumnale, *brings thoughts of spring as the naked stalks push through the carpet of epimedium leaves.*

they lose their leaves to go into dormancy for the summer. Plant *C. hederifolium* with groups of *C. coum* for a continuous flow of flowers for months. The autumn flowers look pretty against a dark background of hellebore leaves, and the cyclamen leaves themselves, mottled with silver, are always beautiful.

Roses in their second flowering have a *fin-de-siècle* air by autumn, and this is when you need fresh flowers and scent. Three shrubs can be nominated, and the first, for colour and fragrance, is *Clerodendrum bungei*. This is a rare shrub, but hardy and beautiful. It has dark, furrowed foliage with a veiling of purple, and in early autumn its large domes of deep pink, scented blossom dominate a late border. It will sucker freely, moving into herbaceous plantings, but as it grows strongly upwards and outwards, it seems not to do much harm. At Hadspen House, Somerset, in the west of England, it has been combined with the

Startling cascades of magenta leaves and decorative bright blue berries appear on Clerodendrum trichotomum *var.* fargesii *in autumn.*

Californian poppy, *Romneya coulteri*, which in late summer produces huge white discs of papery poppy flowers. Its foliage is silver grey and tall and it too suckers, so the combination of dark and light in leaf and flower is serendipitous.

The clerodendrum has an equally lovely relative for the autumn border. *C. trichotomum* is a strong shrub, with white, very fragrant flowers enclosed in maroon calyces, which appear first in late summer but go on well into autumn, when their greater glory appears. The flowers develop into umbels of bright blue seedheads, still with their colourful calyces. This is the ideal shrub to underplant with a collection of cyclamen.

It is difficult to keep away from yellow for long in autumn, and one of the most attractive yellow-flowered shrubs is *Bupleurum fruticosum*, shrubby hare's ear, the only shrubby species of a large genus. Most of the species flower in late summer and the flowers of the herbaceous species, like *B. falcatum* and *B. angulosum*, were once described as 'better than Fabergé jewels'. *B. fruticosum* is one of the best evergreen shrubs for exposed beds. Its gleaming, jade green leaves are quietly elegant all the year, but in early autumn umbels of blossom that have been promising for weeks, suddenly become starred with bright yellow. It leans into other shrubs or makes a fountain of foliage if isolated in a flower bed. It makes a wonderful support for a soft, pliable rose – 'Mme Alfred Carrière' will always oblige by flowering for the second time with the bupleurum, and it sprays its white flowers elegantly into the great mass of yellow flower.

SILVER AND GOLD

Foliage, whether flaming or sea-green, is one of the most important elements of autumn. This is when the great variegated and layered *cornus* species are really quite outstanding.

Both *Cornus controversa* 'Variegata' and *C. alternifolia* 'Argentea' are like huge, tiered wedding cakes although they take many years to build up their strange structure. They are ideal planted in a bed where they can be surrounded by low-growing perennials that allow their architectural structure to be seen. *C. controversa* 'Variegata' has oval leaves heavily marked with cream, and *C. alternifolia* 'Argentea' has smaller, curled leaves that shimmer in sunlight. Both need a dark background to bring out their sparkling qualities, but they both have the spectacular presence needed to create drama in the autumn border. These plants are difficult to propagate, hard to find and often expensive, but they are well worth the trouble.

Easy to buy, easy to grow and much cheaper, but just as slow in building up its structure, is *Euonymus fortunei* 'Silver Queen'. This is a much underrated shrub because it stays tiny for so long, but it slowly spreads out to make a great dome of whitened foliage. The white flowers appear in spring, but it rarely bears the glamorous pink-shelled fruits. It is utterly beautiful as a background for *Hydrangea macrophylla* 'Ayesha', which is a most distinct and unusual cultivar because it has much better leaves than most of the mop-head hydrangeas, which are often rather dull and boring. 'Ayesha' has bold, glossy green leaves, and the flowers are thick-petalled, substantial and each one on the umbel is like a china blue pearlized thimble.

Variegated yuccas come into their own in autumn. They are excellent plants for creating a focal point in the corner of a border surrounded by clipped box. The dark green *Yucca gloriosa* 'Variegata' is the hardiest of the genus. It sends out small runners of new, spiky plants in time so that a group is built up. The flowers appear early in autumn, outstanding great steeples of white bells, but unfortunately, the parent plant often dies after flowering, although it has usually built up into quite a colony by that time and so the gap does not last long.

Silver and gold variegation is also found among the irises. One of the most noticeable in autumn is *Iris foetidissima* 'Variegata', which has clean, striking foliage and pale lilac flowers in summer. If you are lucky, seed pods will burst open to reveal huge clusters of orange seeds. Sadly, although this happens regularly with the plain *Iris foetidissima*, which makes it an excellent autumn plant, it rarely happens with the variegated form.

OUT TO GRASS

Herbaceous plants that flower late but that look good all through the year are few and far between. Ornamental grasses, on the other hand, retain their structure until they are cut down in spring, often looking magical when covered with hoar frost. They alleviate the heaviness of evergreens, and their narrow leaves and feathery flowers are always graceful. One drawback is that they can be a problem to place in the traditional flower bed; try *Miscanthus sinensis* cultivars planted with hydrangeas – *M. sinensis* 'Variegatus', a tall fountain of white and silver leaves, would look wonderful with the *Hydrangea* 'Ayesha' planting described above.

The most difficult plants to place are the pampas grasses. They all flower in autumn, with great plumes of silver and gold, but they are huge and overwhelming. *Cortaderia selloana* 'Aurealineata' (syn. 'Gold Band') produces a huge, swirling pile of long silken leaves but its flowers reach heights of 2.7m (9ft). At the Royal Horticultural Society's Garden, Wisley, pampas grass is shown in a bed with other grasses, where it looks magnificent. On a smaller scale at home, it will be equally good in an island bed, where its shape can be appreciated and

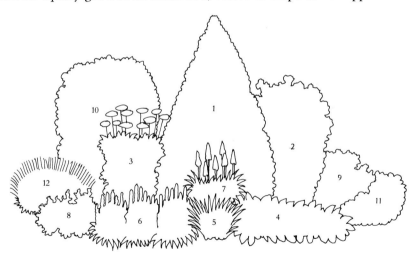

Fig. 15 *A gold and yellow scheme with grasses for autumn colour.*

1 *Ilex aquifolium* 'Pyramidalis'
2 *Angelica archangelica*
3 *Achillea grandifolia*
4 *Hosta* 'Yellow Splash'
5 *Stipa tenuissima*
6 *Kniphofia* 'Little Maid'
7 *Kniphofia* 'Bressingham Comet'
8 *Stachys byzantina* 'Primrose Heron'
9 *Potentilla* 'Elizabeth'
10 *Ligustrum ovalifolium* 'Aureum' and *Clematis macropetala*
11 *Geranium* 'Brookside'
12 *Lavandula angustifolia* 'Hidcote'

surrounded with golden oats, *Stipa tenuissima*, the large oats of *Stipa gigantea*, which dance in front of the solid cortaderia plumes, and a purple-flowered miscanthus. *M. sinensis* var. *purpurascens*, the flame grass, has dark stems, with silvered flowers. Winter frosts change the stems to brilliant orange-red. Surrounded with mounded filigreed silver shrubs of *Santolina pinnata* ssp. *neapolitana*, the whole group shines with lightness.

One of the best autumn grasses is *Stipa tenuissima*, which becomes a waving sea of whitened fronds and is magnificent in a quiet planting of foliage (see Fig. 15). Against a background of a yellow-berried holly, with yellow-splashed hostas, primrose-painted stachys, kniphofias in cream and gold and yellow-leaved privet, it makes a late sunshine picture.

Stipa gigantea is a magnificent plant for a corner where its skirts of shining, dark green leaves can spread out to support the soaring oats flowers. If possible, plant one where sunlight will shine through it to turn every blade to gold.

Leaves do not get much bluer than those of the blue wheat grass, *Elymus magellanicum* (syn. *Agropyron magellanicum*). Its iridescent foliage is outstanding in autumn under the jagged silver leaves of *Cynara cardunculus*, the huge ornamental cardoon, whose giant purple thistle heads burst open in late summer. Equally blue is *Helictotrichon sempervirens*, one of the easiest grasses to place in a mixed border. It grows into a spiky 60cm (2ft) hemisphere, surrounded with shooting stars of blue flowers. It lives happily with glaucous hostas 'Blue Angel', 'Halcyon' or 'Hadspen Blue'.

SILVER STALWARTS

Silver-leaved plants lighten borders, act as full stops between coloured flowers that might clash and are always graceful foliage plants. Many have to be cut hard back in spring, because the new foliage that results is the most intensely silver. They prefer hot, dry situations, and so they should be planted in fully exposed beds and arid edges. Silver plants hate too much wet, and the plump, hairy leaves of plants such as stachys and salvia will become soggy grey messes. The finer leaves are happy in most weathers, however. *Achillea* 'Taygetea' has ferny, silver-green foliage and very pale sulphur flowers, whose colour bleaches in the autumn to palest silver-beige. Even better is *Achillea* 'Moonshine', which has finely cut, almost white leaves, which glimmer in the autumn sunshine.

One of the finest mounds of silver foliage is created by *Centaurea cineraria* ssp. *cineraria*, which is an airy mass of white ferns. It will put up with a certain amount of frost, but winter rains will often deal it a savage blow. It is easy to grow from cuttings, rooted in early autumn, and it is well worth a bit of effort. It looks effective with white annual nicotiana and with hazy *Verbena bonariensis*, whose 1.8m (6ft) stems will tower over it with a shower of blue flowers for extra contrast.

The beloved old lamb's tongue or rabbit's ears of cottage gardens is one of the best edgers, carpeters and corner plants. *Stachys olympica* has silver-felted leaves and it roots to form a mat all along its equally furry stems so is very easily propagated almost leaf by leaf. It is the ideal plant for a quick effect on newly cleared ground and is easily pulled up and moved elsewhere when you find something better.

The leaves of *Stachys byzantina* (syn. *S. olympica*) have a certain solidity, and they make silver, shadowed clumps rather than the flat, silky patterns that some of the older cultivars tended to produce. It makes an excellent edger for roses, where there is space for it to show its true worth.

The huge, curving, grey, divided leaves of the cardoon, *Cynara cardunculus*, are at their best in autumn, as are those of the silver artemisias. *A.* 'Powis Castle', which contrasts so effectively with the cardoon, is vigorous and has abundant, finely cut filamented foliage. It forms enormous plants, which look like grey clouds from a distance. These two giants, planted with a silver variegated form of *Ligustrum ovalifolium*, a fine version of the common privet, make a magnificent centrepiece for a long border. Add a couple of mallows and some deep pink hollyhocks for a fine effect from late summer throughout autumn. The mallows should include a *Lavatera* 'Barnsley', with its white pink-eyed showers of flower that are borne until frost. For the front of the group it is worth seeking out *Malva sylvestris* 'Primley Blue', which is a refined version of the common weed. It creeps along the ground from a woody rootstock and is smothered with cornflower blue flowers, which again last until frost.

Artemisias, which are also known as lad's love, southernwood, old man and wormwood, are a huge group of plants, and there is one for nearly every situation in the garden. *A. absinthium* 'Lambrook Silver' is a subshrub, with finely

Silver plants are at their best as late summer turns into autumn. Artemisia ludoviciana *weaves its way through this border of purple phlox and grey acanthus.*

divided and silvered foliage, which throws out thread–like silver stems of insignificant flowers. If it is cut back as it flowers, new silver leaves appear to flourish right through autumn.

A. aborescens 'Faith Raven' has finely cut and filigreed silver stems and minute leaves, which shine in mist and accentuate the yellow leaves of hostas. *A. ludoviciana* can be cut back as it flowers because its stems are lax and they tend to overlay more delicate plants. In addition, the flowers are generally thought to be uninspiring, but in its best forms the flowers are silvered spires on silver-furred stems at about 90cm (3ft). Against a dark yew hedge, with mats of *Stachys byzantina* at its feet, a carpet of the green whorled woodruff *Galium odoratum* (syn. *Asperula odorata*) to weave into it and domes of *Santolina incana* or *S. pinnata* ssp. *neapolitana* to contrast their discipline with the rampant artemisia, it creates a picture that lasts into midwinter.

There are two small, ground-hugging artemisias that paint the soil with silver. *A. stelleriana*, which does well in shade, has startlingly white leaves that look as if they have been cut out of silver felt, while *A. schmidtiana* is the most fragile-looking silky puff of a plant. It has little whorls of very fine silver leaves, which look as if they would blow away in a strong wind. It is, however, totally hardy and very tough. It will grow and shine in the most inhospitable places, even under a huge *Chamaecyparis leylandii*, where the soil is absolutely bone dry.

Anthemis punctata ssp. *cupaniana* is common, easy but so pretty in its delicate tracery of leaves that it makes one of the best edgings for large beds and borders. It spreads quickly from the tiniest pieces stuck in the ground in spring and it flowers profusely, with large white daisies held stiffly upright over its prostrate foliage. Its thick, downy leaves, which hold points of low light all over their hairy surfaces, are sublime in autumn sunshine following a hot dry summer.

Wetness and cold grey skies do not do a lot for *Salvia argentea*, but in the right conditions it makes a fine feature plant for the front of a border. It forms a basal clump of amazing leaves, covered with white wool. The flowers, which appear in late summer, are borne on long, branching stems and look like powder puffs of angora flowers. Next to it and revelling in the same conditions and contrasting the wool with silver thread could be *Artemisia alba* 'Canescens', which is quite distinctive in form and covered with the laciest of grey foliage in autumn, when it sends up wisps of silver to hold tiny yellow flowers.

In all these ghostly shades, the blooms of *Rosa* 'Iceberg', as fresh in their second flowering as first, stand out like pearlized beacons. Surround them with annual white nicotianas, and, as taller accents, use *Eupatorium rugosum* and *Artemisia lactiflora*. Both are good verticals to contrast with too much roundness. *E. rugosum*, the mist flower or white snakeroot, grows to 1.2m (4ft) and has corymbs of white flowers borne over fresh green leaves. The artemisia is not silver, like most of its relatives, but darkest, strongest green. It is nicknamed the white mugwort, and it flowers in late summer with spires and sprays of tiny white flowers. It has a strange new variant, called *A. lactiflora* Guizho Group, which has erect mahogany stems and deeply cut, almost black foliage, which throws the creamy flowers into strong relief. A truly spectacular plant.

BLACK LEAVES

Black foliage has become fashionable, and black and white gardens may be the next fashion. A bed of *Papaver orientale* 'Black and White', *Artemisia lactiflora* Guizho Group and *Anthriscus sylvestris* 'Ravenswing', which is a very fine, dark, almost black-leaved form of cow parsley, although with much more delicate and refined white flowers, would be striking. There are very dark geraniums, like *Geranium phaeum* 'Mourning Widow', to keep the scheme going for much of the summer. It would truly come into its own in autumn with *Cosmos atrosangineus*, the chocolate flower from Mexico, to add a delicious scent and masses of tiny, dahlia-like flowers. In warm sites it may overwinter, but it is simple to dig it up and keep it in a paper bag until spring. Recently, the cosmos has become available in the form of inexpensive plug plants in spring, and this is a good way to start a collection. *Ophiopogon planiscapus* 'Nigrescens' is the blackest of all black plants. By autumn it will have spread into a mound of overlapping black blades like thick grass and have tiny black berries all over it.

Gleditsia triacanthos 'Rubylace' (see Fig. 16) is the perfect partner for the black-foliaged plants. It has deep purple foliage – as, in truth do most of the 'black' plants – with dancing lights of red, and in its light shade the cimicifugas,

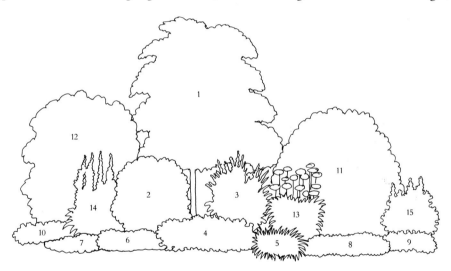

Fig. 16 *A bold scheme for autumn using dark flowers and foliage.*

1 *Gleditsia triacanthos* 'Rubylace'
2 *Artemisia lactiflora* Ghizou group
3 *Cimicifuga simplex* 'Brunette'
4 *Sedum spectabile* 'Indian Chief'
5 *Ophiopogon planiscapus* 'Nigrescens'
6 *Polemonium carneum*
7 *Viola* 'Molly Sanderson'
8 *Viola riviniana* Purpurea group
9 *Ajuga reptans* 'Burgundy Glow'
10 *Ajuga reptans* 'Braunherz'
11 *Cotinus coggygria* 'Royal Purple' and *Clematis viticella*
12 *Hydrangea villosa*
13 *Monarda* 'Vintage Wine'
14 *Penstemon* 'Merlin', *P.* 'Burgundy', *P.* 'Blackbird'
15 *Anthriscus sylvetris* 'Ravenswing'

artemisias, ajugas and anthiriscus all look much blacker. Lighten the scene with green plants with purple flowers – several penstemons have good colours, and the combination of *Polemonium carneum*, with its lilac flowers, and the black-flowered viola is quite heart-stopping. The ophiopogon is one of the best edgers available.

The ophiopogon is a member of the lily family, as is the strange *Liriope muscari*, which is one of the glories of autumn. They make good partners, and planted together they look like exotic marbled grass. Liriope, too, has broad leaves, which grow into strong-centred fountains. Suddenly violet-mauve pokers, just like spring-flowering muscari, shoot up and flower for weeks. There is a white form, *L. muscari* var. *alba*.

Hebe pimeleöides 'Quicksilver' reaches its most intensely steely silver colour by the end of summer, and its sprays of tiny pewter leaves will have reached out by 30cm (12in) or more. It looks brilliant combined with bergenias in a mass planting at the edge of an island bed. The dark green, gradually reddening leaves of the bergenia throw the sparkling hebe into high relief. Add groups of *Nandina domestica*, the sacred bamboo of China, which has lance-shaped, dark green leaves which gradually turn scarlet in autumn and stay on until spring. In warm climates it bears red fruit at the same time. A red-leaved berberis would look as good, and drifts of a golden grass, *Deschampsia cespitosa* 'Bronze Veil', could be planted to infiltrate at different points where its seed heads would trail into the coloured foliages.

Some gardeners prefer actual flowers to seedheads and for them *Gaura lindheimeri* is the answer. It is one of those gauzy flowers with almost transparent stalks, which give the same airy impression as grass. It would make an excellent replacement for the grass. Although it is tall – 1m (3ft) – it has flimsy stems and entrancing cream and pink flowers, which float airily above low-growing edging plants. It is ideal for a sheltered place, for stakes would spoil the ethereal outline. Plant it so that it dances over small, delicate ground-covering subjects and quiet flowerers, like *Omphalodes verna*, whose own pretty blue and white flowers appear in spring.

PLANNING FOR AUTUMN

It is all too easy to fall into the trap of having too many summer or spring flowers together, and they become passengers in autumn. Always plan to have flowers of each season in a group if possible. Planning for autumn leads you quite naturally that way.

One of the best roses in autumn for its glossy green leaves, which gradually turn to butter yellow, is *Rosa rugosa* 'Alba', although all the rugosas are good. Some people prefer the pale pink single flowers of 'Frau Dagmar Hastrup'. *R. rugosa* 'Alba' has single white flowers all summer, and they turn into huge hips, like scarlet tomatoes, which hang on as long as the birds allow. Plant it in front of a group of *Rosa moyesii*, which has cerise pink flowers in summer and, in autumn, immense, flagon-shaped hips, which hang in great apricot-coloured showers. Nearby, group hydrangeas, which have balled or lace-cap flowers that are lovely in late summer but best as they turn bronzed and sea-green when the leaves fall. *Geranium wallichianum* starts into flower late and will trail pinky-blue flat faces over the shrubs until the first frosts. Plant the geranium into a group of earlier flowering plants, like polemonium because *G. wallichianum* 'Buxton's Variety' has a small centre from which all the long growths arise, unlike a normal geranium which makes a clump.

The architectural foliage of cimicifuga, the bugbane, makes an interesting textural contrast with these plants. Cimicifuga needs a good, deep, preferably moist soil, but once it is established it is easy, hardy and there is nothing quite like it in autumn. It grows 1–2.7m (3–9ft) tall and makes strong vertical accents with its white spikes. *C. simplex* 'White Pearl' has bottle-brush spires, soaring to 1.5m (5ft), which are dramatic but containable. At its feet, and to weave with the geranium into the shrub planting, do not overlook nepeta. The little white variety that is fashionable now is not such a good grower as the older, more vigorous *N.* 'Six Hills Giant', which grows strongly, flowering happily under the roses in their midsummer heyday. Cut it back in after the first flowers have faded, and it will quickly be covered in cloudy bright blue flowers again. It will flower again quite well even if it is not pruned, but it will have sprawled rather untidily by that time.

All these subjects will flower bravely on until the first frosts turn the garden into a bonfire.

CHAPTER 6

WHEN WINTER COMES

W INTER IS THE TIME when beds and borders shaded in high summer by trees and the luxuriant growth of shrubs come into their own. They are often close to the house or in sheltered parts of the garden. Here the scented plants of winter revel in the shelter and draw in early flying insects to pollinate them – it has to be a very strong scent to attract an intrepid bee or beetle. Plants that look and smell good in the winter are best grouped together perhaps in a border close to the house. Even in rough weather, the back and front doors are always used. They are the two places you will see every day, while beds further from the house may be viewed only intermittently, and the great bonus of winter is the architectural form of many of its special stars that make a border interesting.

Island beds need a central feature with height, which is often a tree or a group of shrubs. For winter interest choose a tree with lovely bark and group around it the great flowering evergreens of winter and decorate the edges with hellebores. Evergreen shrubs come first to give a backbone to the planting, to furnish the house walls and to give a lustrous look to spring and summer flowers. Tuck in one or two of the barer shrubs that flower brilliantly but look like a forest of sticks unless they are carefully sited and drape them with summer flowering climbers for later colour. Add scads of the little flowers that take no notice of harsh frost and snow apart from bending their heads for a few days. These flowers of winter are not fleeting and ephemeral like those of summer, but seem to last for weeks on end.

TREE FEATURES

Where space is at a premium or in a larger area to create a focal point, a tree with winter interest is the perfect choice. In the summer there are other delights to attract the eye, and the tree can always become host to a spectacular climber. An evergreen tree is the obvious answer, and if it can be clipped to keep it in order so much the better. Trees of all kinds should be avoided in beds near to the house because their roots can do much damage to fragile foundations. The cypress, laurel and box, which have been classic elements since the Romans designed the first civilized gardens, can be trained or clipped to fit a wall space and always look smartly architectural.

Frost glistens on the filigreed silhouettes of a herbaceous border, seen against the backdrop of a disciplined yew hedge, making as beautiful and as interesting a picture as the same border in the midst of high summer.

Dark green foliage in the depths of winter is warming if it is matt and coniferous, but if you choose a light-reflecting, broad-leaved evergreen you inject a shining element into the garden. *Arbutus unedo*, the strawberry tree, is the greatest of all winter-flowering and fruiting beauties. It grows to about 2.7m (9ft) in ten years, so it is a very small tree that will do little harm and only beautify any house. From early autumn into the depths of winter it is covered with panicles of waxy, translucent flowers, and it bears its 'strawberries' at the same time. These hang in pretty, vivid scarlet clusters, tempting the unwise, for they taste of nothing at all. At the same time the current year's flowers are unfolding, each individual like a tiny cluster of lily-of-the-valley but waxy and hanging. *Arbutus* × *andrachnoides* has even better bark and is reputed to be hardier.

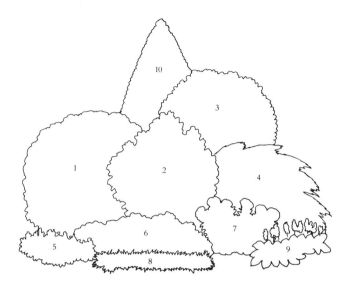

Fig. 17 *A shrub border for winter colour.*

1 *Stachyurus chinensis*
2 *Arbutus unedo*
3 *Viburnum* × *bodnantense* 'Dawn'
4 *Juniperus* × *media* 'Pfitzeriana'
5 *Pachyphragma macrophyllum*

6 *Brachyglottis* Dunedin hybrid 'Sunshine'
7 *Euphorbia characias* ssp. *wulfenii*
8 *Festuca glauca*
9 *Bergenia* 'Wintermärchen'
10 *Taxus baccata* 'Fastigiata'

An arbutus makes a lovely centrepiece for a winter border. But remember, it is always best to plant each border in a small garden for effect throughout the year. The scheme shown in Fig. 17, therefore, includes evergreen and deciduous winter flowering or fruiting shrubs to make a good basis for summer-flowering perennials or annuals, or even for self-seeders like *Meconopsis cambrica*, the Welsh poppy. The many small flowering bulbs, like snowdrops, chionodoxa, scillas and muscaris, will make the early months of the year as bright as a jewel box.

The arbutus will start the flowering season in autumn, and soon the *Stachyrus chinensis* will form its tiny pink-tinged catkins, which echo the colour of the arbutus but contrast in form. *Viburnum* × *bodnantense* 'Dawn' will bear great corymbs of pink blooms from early autumn, and depending on frost, will go on until early spring.

Juniperus × *media* 'Pfitzeriana' has a strong horizontal architectural shape, which will contrast with the upright yew, *Taxus baccata* 'Fastigiata', to give a dominant evergreen impression. Each shrub is complemented by the silver of the brachyglottis and festuca, the shine on the deep red leaves of the bergenia and the clouds of white pachyphragma flowers in late winter.

Holly can be used to make an exciting focus for an island bed of winter treasures. It is traditionally appropriate to the season, but the common holly, *Ilex aquifolium*, is a prickly beast, suited only to hedgerows for the shed leaves are painful for unwary weeding fingers. The variegated cultivars, however, and there are more than 300 hollies from around the world, are unbeatable for colour and a sharply focused shape in winter. *Ilex crenata* 'Shiro-fukurin', which has tiny box-shaped leaves, grows into a neat cone that looks charming in the winter when its tiny berries adorn it, and even better in summer, when a *Clematis texensis* 'Etoile Rose' can be persuaded to twine into it.

Easiest of the hollies and one of the most spectacular is *Ilex altaclarensis* 'Golden King', which has broad, almost spineless leaves, which make it easier to grow in a bed or border, that are green with a yellow margin. For a more subtle effect try *I. altaclarensis* 'Lawsoniana' with smoky gold splashes in the middle of the leaves or *I. aquifolium* 'Handsworth New Silver', which has creamy-white margined leaves and red berries.

Phillyreas are small but handsome evergreen trees with masses of plumy-foliage. When they are placed at the back of a border they look like thunderclouds, with pinpoints of light all over them. They can be trimmed into great globes of green on a strong woody stem, rather like fashionable box balls on stems, but they have a greater presence for a large bed.

DECIDUOUS TREES FOR WINTER OUTLINES

Sorbus cashmiriana is the perfect small tree to highlight a winter bed or border. From mid-autumn onwards it has drooping clusters of fruits, which, weather permitting, will gleam like white china beads until late winter. Some years the birds need them early and they are gone long before winter ends, but the birds take white berries last, and a sorbus with red berries stands little chance of keeping them into the winter. Pink fruits have nearly as long a life as the white, and *Sorbus vilmorinii* and *S. hupehensis* have the added bonus of dark purplish bark and scarlet resting buds of the new leaves waiting to escape in spring. The fruit on both species hangs in large clusters, turning from pink-tinged to white over the winter.

Birch trees are obvious candidates for winter interest, and they look magnificent underplanted with *Cornus alba* 'Sibirica', with its bright red stems. Add several plants of *Helleborus foetidus* for an evergreen and lime-flowered ground cover and you have a classic planting.

Look out for unusual birches, but remember not to plant them close to your house, for the roots are greedy and surface-feeding and could damage foundations. As a centrepiece for an island bed, however, there is nothing better than a group of *Betula pendula*, the common silver birch or lady of the woods, but *B. papyrifera*, the paper bark birch, which Native Americans used for their canoes, is much more exciting. It has very white bark, and it pays to take a bucket of soapy water with a scrubbing brush and give its trunk a spring clean once a year to get a clear, sparkling texture.

Betula utilis var. *jacquemontii* is a medium sized tree with attractively peeling bark and dazzling white stems. It does not have the fault of the common birch, in that the trunk does not become serrated and blackened in middle age.

Not all birches have silver bark. *Betula albosinensis* var. *septentrionalis* is a beautiful tree with pink and red bark covered with a glaucous bloom. Take off all the lower branches as the tree gains height to give yourself a long stretch of the trunk. *Betula ermanii* is almost apricot through a silvery veil of paper-thin bark. But beware: birches are greedy, they take a lot of food and moisture away from any flowering plants you place nearby. Remember to feed generously under birches and provide as much water as you can.

Acers are small trees that have a lot of winter interest. Some have stripy bark – *A. davidii* has lovely striated green and white bark; *A. grosseri* is one of the most beautiful of the snake-bark maples and is strikingly striped; *A. rufinerve* and *A. pensylvanicum* are equally attractive.

But *A. palmatum* 'Senkaki' is in a class of its own. Known as the coral bark maple it is a small tree – it can be kept in a pot for several years – with the most astonishingly pretty red stems. It has a slight trunk and many branches all with a scarlet sheen. All winter long it is like a flaming torch and is a wonderful accent by the front door. In spring it has shrimp pink leaves, which eventually become green, but always have a reddish cast, and in the autumn it fires up just like a bonfire. This tree would make a winter border on its own.

Acer griseum, the paperback maple, is one of the most beautiful of all small trees. The bark on the trunk and main branches flakes and curls back to reveal the cinnamon-coloured underbark. It is an entrancing sight, especially underplanted with snowdrops and aconites.

Two cherries should also be considered for the winter border – in fact, you should try to make room for them somewhere in the garden whatever your planting scheme. *Prunus serrula* has the most dramatic bark. It shines like mahogany ribbon and peels back to reveal layer after layer of this lovely fabric. Unfortunately, it has rather uninspiring leaves and very ordinary flowers, but you can, sometimes, find a *P. serrula* with a *P. sargentii* head grafted on to it. Then you get the bonus of the loveliest of all cherry flowers in soft pink showing at the same time as the young bronze-red leaves. In autumn it has glorious orange and crimson tints in its falling leaves, which leave a wonderful carpet on the ground as they fall.

Even more cheerful is *P.* × *subhirtella* 'Autumnalis', which is showered with tiny white flowers for the whole winter. Against a dark yew hedge there is no better winter picture, and, except in very bad weather, there are sheets of blossom from early winter into the spring. If the winter is very bad, the flowers hold back and appear happily almost into summer.

WINTER-FLOWERING SHRUBS

The evergreen winter-flowering shrubs are some of the most architectural plants, and they are indispensable in giving a border or bed a good structure. Used in groups under one of the small trees that star in the cold weather, they can make a quiet heart for an interesting border year-round. Box and yew are the perfect winter evergreens. A garden of clipped and shaped shrubs, combined with fastigiate conifers and stone ornaments, is the perfect picture for deep winter doldrums. Even a little line of clipped box with perhaps a ball or cone will furnish your garden through the bare times.

A shrub that should always be grown where it can be seen from a window is the mahonia. It is striking at all times, but particularly good in winter. *Mahonia × media* 'Charity', 'Lionel Fortescue' or 'Winter Sun' are majestic evergreens. They have lovely, tasselled, pale lemon flowers from late autumn until after midwinter. After they have flowered, cut some of the stems well back to get better foliage and to help prevent the shrubs from developing a gaunt appearance. The flowers are one of the exciting things about the mahonia, but if the stems are not cut, magnificent blue berries follow. The more common mahonias – *M. japonica*, the Bealei Group and *M. aquifolium* – are all good shrubs for the winter garden, and they have long, racemes of clear yellow, sweetly scented flowers.

If you have suitable soil, the lime-hating rhododendrons, camellias and pieris are the finest evergreen shrubs of all. For those with acid soil and a high rainfall, there is a huge choice of flower colour, size and magnificent leaf to choose from. All three of these shrubs can be grown in containers as long as they are given lime-free compost, and if you live in the drier areas of the world, the only way to grow them is in tubs, where their moisture intake can be monitored.

WINTER MAINSTAY

The viburnums, both evergreen and deciduous, are a mainstay of the winter garden. The deciduous species are the angular shrubs that flower extravagantly and fragrantly in the depths of winter but look rather boring and plain in high summer. Plant them at the back of the border where the flowers will be seen over a sheet of evergreen foliage and will be forgotten in late springtime. Some of them make excellent hosts for vigorous clematis, particularly the *viticellas*, which will climb to a great height in summer.

Viburnum × bodnantense 'Dawn' is the best of these rather ungainly shrubs. It will grow 3m (10ft) tall and 2.4m (8ft) thick if you let it, but it will flower just as prolifically if you prune it carefully. The flower clusters are huge, vivid pink and smell so sweetly they make the winter worthwhile. A 'Dawn' seen in full flower across a bare garden is an astonishing sight for deep winter.

Viburnum tinus, the old fashioned laurustinus, is an evergreen from the Mediterranean, and it needs a sheltered spot to prevent winter scorching in areas exposed to cold winter winds. It hardly ever seems to be without a flower, but its great glory begins in autumn, when every stem has a corymb of pink-budded white blossom. If it were a difficult plant or just collected from some exotic land, we would all want it. As it is, it often gets the worst place in a garden. Try it in the corner of a bed, where its voluminous growth will spread out like skirts and it will hold its flat heads of lacy flowers until the middle of spring at the least. It thrives in shade, so it can be grown under a tree.

Daphnes are among the most highly scented shrubs, but they are mostly spring flowering. The exception is *Daphne bholua* 'Gurkha', which originates from the Himalayas. It will grow to 1.8m (6ft) tall and at the end of winter it will be a mass of gloriously scented pink-white flowers. Each flower has a purple stain on the outside of the petals. It is fairly easy to grow and will put up with some sun and some shade. In the right place it could be the perfect winter plant, but there is some question about its hardiness, and it will not survive the most severe, constantly freezing weather. *D. mezereum*, the most often seen, sweet-scented deciduous shrub flowers in midwinter with tiny purple or white flowers, which are massed up its fanned branches. Sometimes it is loaded with scarlet and orange fruit afterwards, and these can be sown. There are often several seedlings growing around each plant, which should be potted up so that the parent plant can be replaced in due course. They are not long-lived. The leaves of *D. odora* 'Aureomarginata' have creamy-white edges, and almost pink flowers are borne in late winter. It is quite hardy and always lovely in the border.

Danae racemosa is a charming, small evergreen, which is happy in deep shade where its gleaming leaves shine out. This graceful shrub is known as the Alexandrian laurel because the Greeks wove wreaths for conquering heroes from its leaves. Arching sprays of narrow, polished foliage spring from a centre crown. New lush growth, rather like juicy asparagus tips, pushes through the soil in spring to replace the old stems, which should be cut away, for they eventually brown and spoil the shrub. It looks particularly fine combined with sarcococcas and the huge-leaved fatsia when all three evergreens weave into a green tapestry under a conifer.

The fatsia is often grown as a houseplant, but it makes an excellent hardy shrub and will grow to tree-like proportions against a sheltered wall. *Fatsia japonica* has very large, polished, dark green, palmate leaves, which look almost sub-tropical. In a very heavy frost they bow down from the stems, looking as if they would break and drop, but as soon as the air warms, the leaves rise back into position. In early winter panicles of milk-white, globular flower heads are held between the leaves and they, too, look fragile in the frost but somehow survive to turn into balls of black berries.

Both the fatsia and the danae look good together in a winter planting (see Fig. 18). The sinuous, shining wands of the danae sway away from the striking presence of the fatsia and are highlighted by the sword-shaped leaves of the iris that will bear tall stems of orange berries in great abundance through autumn and winter. Birds leave them until there is very little else to eat – flower arrangers are the great predators of the iris berries. The dramatic tall grass, *Miscanthus sinensis* 'Variegatus' will be straw-coloured by late winter, but it will retain its good structure. Cut it down hard in early spring so that the strong, new growths of silvered blades grow up in the summer.

Pachysandra terminalis makes a lovely contrast with the iris, and the large-leaved vinca is magnificent next to the orange berries as is the ivy's variegated leaves. Cut the vinca's yellow-splashed foliage hard back in late winter before the plant can spread out further than you need.

Deciduous shrubs with good outlines and resting winter buds are a foil for all the evergreens. Magnolias are especially impressive when bare. *Magnolia × soulangeana* is particularly good, its bare branches making a strong woven outline against the sky, and the already-swelling fat buds will be loading each one down by late winter.

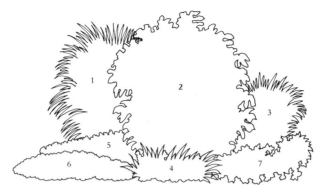

Fig. 18 *A winter planting with strong, contrasting foliage.*

1 *Miscanthus sinensis* 'Variegatus'

2 *Fatsia japonica*

3 *Danae racemosa*

4 *Iris foetidissima*

5 *Pachysandra terminalis*

6 *Vinca major* 'Variegata'

7 *Hedera helix* ssp. *helix* 'Glacier'

The hammamelis or witch hazels from China and America make large shrubs with spreading branches that ascend in a strange way. They are best in island beds where their full beauty can be seen from all sides. Their bare stems have a soft, buff down, and their tiny flowers are jewel-like as they form throughout the summer. Then in winter they burst forth. Often the first thing you notice is the pervasive scent of sweetness – it is said to be reminiscent of cowslips – and then there is a gold shading to the shrub. Some cultivars have brassy yellow flowers which are outstanding in the winter landscape, but the best, *Hamamelis* × *intermedia* 'Pallida', is a soft primrose colour. 'Jelena' is one of the best of the coppery-red cultivars, but they are all beautiful. Every year new cultivars are raised and named, and if you have space, a little grove of them is a true delight in late winter. Underplant the witch hazel with primroses and violets, which will often flower at the same time with solitary flowers – not the great cumulus of blossom of spring – that will match the ethereal slightness of the witch hazel. Add the evergreen whorls of *Euphorbia robbiae*, a handsome ground cover, for an elegant but easy winter picture. There are some magnificent euphorbias, but *E. robbiae* and *E. characias* ssp. *wulfenii* are the best in winter. *E.c.* ssp. *wulfenii* starts to produce its great lime green heads over whorled blue-green stems in late winter, but it is always a telling picture in the garden landscape. At 1.2m (4ft) tall it is a dramatic accent for winter plantings.

If your beds or borders are not large enough to take a wide-spreading witch hazel, try a *Cornus mas* 'Variegata'. In fifteen years it reaches about 2.4m (8ft), but it is always fine and delicate. In midwinter its naked twigs are covered with

The subtle bronze-coloured flowers on the bare stems of Hamamelis × intermedia *'Jelena' stand out against the domes of evergreen heathers and contrast well with the silvery sheen of the branches of* Rubus biflorus.

small yellow flowers, and when this happens it is a dazzling sight against winter evergreens. In summer the leaves are conspicuously margined with white; in autumn it has fruit like little cherries which are edible, so it earns its keep at all times of the year.

Sarcococca hookeriana var. *dignya* and *S. confusa* are the sweetest smelling winter evergreens. They have distinguished foliage, narrow but shining, which sparkles intensely in late winter when the tiny white flowers hidden under the foliage pierce the air with perfume. It looks good grown as small shrubs in beds on each side of a doorway, where its quiet elegance will be fine all year. You have only to open the door in the depths of winter to be assailed by scent.

CONIFERS

Conifers are contentious. Some garden designers loathe them, and older gardeners often hate variegated ones, which they regard as vulgar. Nevertheless, one or two well-chosen plants will brighten the borders in winter and make a colourful foil for spring and summer flowers. Most conifers, even if they are sold as 'miniature', get tall and wide with age, and the best choice is yew, *Taxus* spp., for you can clip and train it. A yew hedge is perfect for showing off flowering plants, and it is always a marvellous piece of winter furniture.

The blue conifers are beautiful but difficult to place. Their colours look almost artificial, and most of them grow into enormous columns and spires. The smooth *Cupressus arizonica* is attractive, although it slowly grows into an enormous tree. The foliage is greyish-green with a blue tinge, and it has attractive peeling red bark that goes purple with age. *Cupressus arizonica* var. *glabra* is the tree to look out for – when it is fairly young it has the most glamorous cones. Unlike most of the very blue conifers, it tones easily with flowering shrubs and roses.

One or two golden conifers sprinkled among evergreen shrubs will lighten the landscape, and all small conifers leaven a planting of deciduous shrubs. Look out for cultivars with golden, silver or creamy variegated foliage. Again the best are often yews – *Taxus baccata* 'Fastigiata' is a lovely dark green tree, but almost better is *T. baccata* 'Aureomarginata', which is known as the golden Irish yew. Its leaves are stained with gold, and it grows into an impressive spire or it can be clipped into a narrow cylinder. *T. baccata* 'Standishii' is very slow-growing and has brilliantly whorled yellow leaves; *T. baccata* 'Aurea' is a large, compact shrub with golden yellow leaves that can be clipped into a large mound to mark a corner; and *T. baccata* 'Dovastoniana' has distinct, wide-spreading tiers of long branches and smaller branches that weep downwards, it is available in green or gold forms.

FLOWERS OF WINTER

Many of the flowers that remain in the garden in the depths of winter will be left over flowers of summer. The first true flower of winter, in status as well as time, is the snowdrop. There are many species and named cultivars – some gardeners have as many as a hundred – but drifts of the common *Galanthus nivalis* look beautiful for many weeks from midwinter onwards. They lie like fleece throughout bare borders, bringing the first exciting indication of the stirring underground. Snowdrops may be planted by the hundred among shrubs and herbaceous perennials. Their foliage is delicate and disappears as suddenly as it arrives to make beds look attractively green even when the flowers fade. A few snowdrop bulbs will soon multiply so that in only a few years you will have great drift of them.

Snowdrop bulbs are often offered for sale in autumn by mail order merchants. However, because they hate to be dried off, many of these bulbs come to nothing when they are planted. It is far better to look out for the advertisements that appear in early spring in the gardening magazines for bulbs 'in the green'. They are sold in bundles of fifty or a hundred, singles as well as the less common double, and they look rather like bunches of salad onions with their long, limp green leaves, but the tiny bulbs are plump and firm. Plant them at once. At this time of the year it is easy to see exactly where you need winter white to set off your sparkling evergreens.

As your own groups of bulbs grow bigger, flowering time is also the time to divide and replant them. It can even be done when the snowdrops are in full bloom if you are impatient and long to see the results at once. Dig up a clump carefully, divide into several little groups and replant them at once just where you want them. Make sure they do not dry out and within days you will think snowdrops have carpeted your bed for ever. Do this year after year and you will have wave after wave of white. Snowdrops also seed easily, so leave heads to develop and you will find tiny hair-like seedlings all around each year to add to your family of bulbs.

A group of mahonias, perhaps a tall *M.* × *media* 'Charity' with its shooting stars of palest yellow flowers, underplanted with the lowly *M. aquifolium* and its promise of buttercup yellow snubby flowers yet to come, surrounded by a sea of snowdrops makes a strong winter picture for a corner bed near the house. Add groups of white *Helleborus orientalis* or *H. foetidus* swathed with *Vinca minor F. alba*, with its neat ground-covering green leaves and white star flowers. Try a variegated vinca with bright blue flowers if you want a more colourful scheme or a decorative white-splashed ivy for a more subtle effect. Snowdrops and hellebore of all varieties can be used in this way to wind through a bed or border to give a permanent winter-flowering base that will grow and increase by seed over the years.

Another bulb that flowers early and often finds its Elizabethan ruffs rimed with frost and snow is the winter aconite, *Eranthis hyemalis*. This ancient plant, with its butter yellow, cupped flowers, first sends up delicate shoots of bronzy green that unfold into mounds of leaves. They will carpet ground that is in deepest shade and will last for several weeks. Like snowdrops, they, too, should be bought 'in the green' and planted while the leaves are still fresh. They like the shade of deciduous trees, but they are sometimes difficult to establish and do not multiply as rapidly as snowdrops. The two planted together make a perfect combination − the spear-like blades of the snowdrop leaves and the delicate nodding bells contrast excitingly with the lusher, roundness of the aconite.

Cyclamen coum is a startling sight in midwinter when the tiny pink and white flowers drift like butterflies under the shade of large trees or shrubs. If they have space to seed freely there will soon be a carpet of colour, and the leaves make sheets of marbled green. Buy them in pots rather than as dry corms − because they are quite difficult to establish once dried out. Always leave them to seed, which they will do in suitable soil, and be careful not to weed the tiny new corms. They are best left to build up strong colonies in the shade where few other plants will thrive.

The cyclamens will grow well in the shade of a *Malus floribunda* (see Fig. 19), which will give an umbrella of blossom to shade them in the spring. They are also lovely grouped with purple or pink forms of *Helleborus orientalis* and interwoven with veils of pink, white or blue *Anemone blanda*. Add a small-leaved

Even while it is still winter, snowdrops, Galanthus nivalis, *bring sparkling highlights to the carpet of* Cyclamen coum.

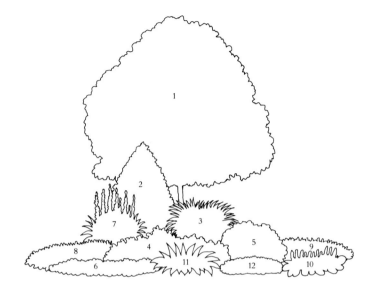

Fig. 19 *A silver and pink winter border.*

1 *Malus floribunda*
2 *Ilex myrtifolia*
3 *Pleioblasus variegatus*
4 *Helleborus orientalis*
5 *Anthemis punctata* ssp. *cupaniana*
6 *Viola riviniana* Purpurea group
7 *Sisyrinchium striatum*
8 *Cyclamen coum*
9 *Cyclamen hederifolium*
10 *Bergenia* 'Silverlight'
11 *Adiantum pedatum*
12 *Sedum* 'Bertram Anderson'

holly – *Ilex myrtifolia* is one of the most elegant, slow-growing species – and lighten the whole with a slow variegated bamboo, which will echo the silvered leaves of the cyclamen. Later in the year, the silver threads of *Anthemis punctata* ssp. *cupaniana* will foam forwards to heighten the effect of the glistening white flowers of *Bergenia* 'Silverlight'. The little fern, *Adiantum pedatum*, will weave into the low-growing, black-leaved *Sedum* 'Bertram Anderson', which is a perfect foil for the purple-leaved *Viola riviniana* and the silver-streaked cyclamen.

Another winter favourite with marbled leaves is *Arum italicum* ssp. *italicum* 'Marmoratum' (syn. A.i. var. *pictum*), which unfurls its first leaves in late autumn from peculiar hooded buds. They display extravagantly under trees or shrubs before they disappear again to be replaced with striking stems of poisonous red berries. They look lovely in a narrow border, where annuals could be planted for summer colour.

For a magical effect, plant a winter jasmine, *Jasmine nudiflorum*, so that it can be trained above the arum to fall down like a fountain. The jasmine is versatile because it can be grown as a shrub, with support, and it makes excellent ground cover. It would thread through the space given over to arum so that the barer moments would be enlivened with its bright green stems. If the stems are trained upwards the flowers make an elegant yellow waterfall, but they look like stars caught in the marbled foliage on the ground. The jasmine flowers for most of the winter and is sweetly scented. Try growing it into and over a magnificent winter foliage subject, an ivy *Hedera colchica* 'Sulphur Heart' (syn. 'Paddy's Pride'). Its golden variegation highlights the pale primrose of the jasmine, and the strong stems of the ivy hold up the frail jasmine. Nearby, plant a *Garrya elliptica*, which has plain green evergreen foliage for most of the year but is suddenly illuminated in winter by tassels of grey and green, which in the cultivar 'James Roof' grow to about 30cm (12in) long. It can be burnt by hard frost and needs the shelter of a wall clad with golden ivy to look its best.

Add a few *Iris unguicularis* (syn. *I. stylosa*) at the foot of this planting. The winter flowering iris – it goes on from winter through to spring in good weather – has delicate blue flowers that will survive frost. If they are taken indoors, every bud will open. These irises like the starved soil they will probably get under an ivy and a jasmine.

HEATHERS AND HELLEBORES

The colourful foliage and bright flowers, many of them borne in winter, make heathers popular and useful. *Erica* × *darleyensis* has pale pink, purple-shadowed flowers throughout winter, and the neat foliage grows in the typically crunchy way. Although some gardeners dislike the fact that the foliage of the thousands of different heather cultivars is similar, great banks of them in winter, under the white stems of birches and with the coloured bark of different cornus trees, is a thrilling spectacle.

Cornus alba 'Sibirica' has particularly good, bright crimson stems, while *C. stolonifera* 'Flaviramea' has glowing yellow bark. One of the best winter plantings incorporating all these is at the Cambridge Botanic Garden, which is like a winter wonderland.

There green hellebores are grown with heathers to make an even stronger foliage contrast. *Helleborus foetidus* is a marvel of dark green dissected leaves surmounted by clusters of pale green bells, and *H. argutifolius* has evergreen jade foliage, sculptured and jagged, with enormous cupped, apple green flowers.

The shining white bells of the Christmas rose, *Helleborus niger*, rarely appear until well into winter, unless the plant is covered with a cloche for weeks. It has been used as the parent for many new hybrids and the interest in these plants is so intense that new ones are eagerly sought. Some now have marbled leaves, and there are new colours and even precious doubles coming along.

H. orientalis, the Lenten rose, comes into flower from winter onwards, and it is very exciting when the first buds appear, often through snow and ice. The flowers are in shades of white, pink, rose and darkest plum, and the latest colour is yellow, but these plants are still rare. Some are almost black, but they are treasured like gold and difficult to obtain. The individual plants make huge

clumps of magnificent foliage, and twenty or thirty buds are not uncommon on mature plants. They look best grown in front of evergreen shrubs such as camellias and mahonias, and the darker forms look good with *Hamamelis* × *intermedia* 'Pallida', with blue pulmonarias and omphalodes, and with tiny blue and white bulbs. Snowdrops in front of the dark flowers look pristine and help to highlight the hellebores, which can disappear into the background. Cyclamen, which are still flowering when the hellebores first appear, are excellent growing among their handsome leaves.

The spotted forms of hellebore are a special joy, but it is the double *H. torquatus* Party Dress Group, that causes crowds to form when the plants appear at flower shows.

The vivid stems of the red-barked dogwood, Cornus alba *'Sibirica', are accentuated by frost and by the contrasting yellow foliage of one of the better golden conifers,* Chamaecyparis lawsoniana *'Winston Churchill'.*

    Hellebores should be given an annual mulch of good, well-made compost and they should be watered in dry weather. Unfortunately, the newer cultivars do not seed around like the easier *H. orientalis*, which is hardy and so beautiful that a drift of them with carpets of wood anemones, *Anemone nemorosa* in soft blues and whites, and scads of *Cyclamen coum* shows that winter has a beauty hardly matched in summer.

CHAPTER 7

MAINTAINING BEDS AND BORDERS

ONCE YOU HAVE PLANTED your beds and borders the hard work starts. If you want a garden crammed with healthy, romantic plants weaving colourfully into each other, it may take several hours of your time each week to maintain. To some people this can be off-putting but many maintenance operations can be relaxing and even enjoyable. The main point to make is that there is no such thing as an easy garden unless it is planted only with evergreens or has a high proportion of concrete.

SPRING

Spring is the busiest time of year for most gardeners, with the weather making decisions for them. Some years it is too wet to walk on the borders without damaging the soil structure. A simple solution is to lay short lengths of wooden planks over the earth to act as pathways.

Spring is the time to rake and feed the top soil, destroy annual weeds and prune any silver shrubs. Many plants can be pruned in early to mid spring. However, in a small garden it may be easier to leave pruning until late spring, so that you can prune everything at once.

Early spring is the best time to move and divide snowdrops (*Galanthus* spp.). This can be done when they are in full bloom. The white flowers will go on blooming even after the clump has been split carefully apart.

At this time also, check for young weeds, such as cow parsley, speedwell and bittercress, which will be easy to deal with now. Take care not to step on emerging bulb leaves, especially tulips, which make an early appearance.

Many tall-growing, weak-stemmed perennials are unable to support themselves when they reach full height. Some can be mixed in with strong-growing, medium sized plants, which provide support, or can lean dramatically into roses and shrubs. Others, however, will need staking and this must be carried out in spring. Use single stakes, such as bamboo canes, for delphiniums and similar plants. For other perennials make a ring of fine bamboo canes and wind them round with string. If you are using wooden or steel supports, put the stake in as soon as the plants start to grow, so that the flower stems pierce upwards through the supports. Keep the support at a lower height than the foliage growth to make sure it is unobtrusive.

Plants have to be moved for all kinds of reasons. They may outgrow their allotted space or just not look right where you originally put them. There are many different views on the best time to move plants; some say autumn, some spring, few advise summer although it is possible for many species. Most plants can be moved at any time if the soil is in good condition, the weather is wet and not too windy, and you take great care with the move. Almost all plants can be moved in late spring. It is obviously better to avoid the need to move plants, particularly the permanent trees and shrubs that give structure to your beds and borders. These will require extra care and regular watering after they have been moved. Perennials and biennials are easier to move and should soon settle in.

SUMMER

If you have thoroughly cleared your borders of perennial weeds in the winter, and mulched them well, you will have minimized the need for summer weeding. However, it is almost impossible to remove all weed seeds from manure or heavy vegetable composts and some weeding needs to be carried out throughout the course of the summer.

Edging the lawns is one of the most important summer jobs and is something that can be combined with weeding. As you cut along with your edging shears or strimmer, your eye is drawn into the borders and you will spot any weeds.

Another summer task is deadheading fading flowers. This encourages many plants to flower again as they are unable to set seed. Cut back to a new leaf or flower bud with secateurs or scissors; do not leave a forest of stalks as this will look unattractive. With some plants, such as hydrangeas, it is best to leave dead flower heads on the plant as they protect the new flower buds forming underneath. Some plants, such as *Salvia superba*, geraniums, *Viola cornuta*, *Centaurea montana* and some phlox will flower for a second time if they are shorn completely to the ground. They soon spring back into growth.

Silver and grey-foliaged plants need exactly the opposite of the care advocated for some of the more colourful garden plants. They loathe manure, need no compost and prefer dry, stony soil. This can make it difficult to combine them with lush roses and perennials, but that is where they often look best. It is easiest to give them the right conditions at the edges of beds and borders. They can be used to fence in the rich feeders into a mini border of their own. The mulches will be kept back from the lawns by the dry barrier. Most silver and grey plants must be kept under control by shearing over in early spring and mid summer. This will also ensure the foliage stays a good colour and provide cutting material which can be rooted directly in the soil in late summer. Lavender (*Lavandula* spp.) should be cut after it has flowered, but never cut into old wood as the plant will rarely regrow. Santolina and *Senecio* 'Sunshine' are usually cut back to a good shape in early summer, and then trimmed in mid summer.

Summer is also the best time to propagate many perennials and tender plants by cuttings. Use a clean, sharp knife to cut a heel or small slip from just below a nose or bud, and push the cutting into a small pot containing half sand and half compost. It is worth trying this with all perennials that are not easy to divide (generally those that make small crowns or grow very slowly) as well as tender plants. If you take cuttings at the end of summer, leave them to overwinter in the original pot; potting-on can cause losses. If cuttings are taken earlier in the summer they can be moved on into larger or separate pots and kept in a cold frame. By autumn they will be sturdy plants.

AUTUMN

Autumn is the time to make mulch using a chipper or shredder. Some things have to be burnt but most prunings and cut down, herbaceous perennials can be turned into mulching material. It must be dry otherwise you will spend ages untangling long green strings from the shredder blades.

Now is also the time to build a good compost heap with the lawn mowings, vegetable matter and dead flowerheads collected over the summer and layered with your shreddings and softer autumn waste material. To this can be added all kinds of household waste, such as fruit and vegetables (not meat or fish), hair, wool, even newspapers and cardboard, which will rot eventually and add to the fibre content.

Bare-rooted trees and shrubs should be planted in autumn. Many container-grown trees and shrubs, such as conifers, can usually be left until spring, when they will get off to a better start as their roots reach out into warm soil. Philadelphus, weigelas, spireas and other tough shrubs are best planted in autumn, when they will enjoy the frequent rains. By the spring they will be well established.

Container-grown shrubs will usually have been kept in a warm tunnel in the nursery. If they are bought in spring they must be hardened for several weeks before planting. Autumn is a good time to give your beds and borders a top-dressing of bonemeal. It is slow acting, organic and provides nutritious phosphorus, but can be expensive if you have a large garden.

Autumn is the best time to take stock of your garden, to go around with a notebook and make plans for the future. At this time of year it is easy to see which plants have taken up too much space, which silver shrubs have become greener because they have too much shade, which trees and shrubs need pruning and lopping to keep them in good shape. Your memory of the garden at its best is still strong and you can note which colour schemes were not successful and decide which ones to adjust to make them even better the following year.

WINTER

Winter is the time to dig new beds and borders. Before doing so remove all perennial weeds and any established perennials you want to keep. Many people now do not like to use weedkillers but for some persistent and pernicious weeds

The reds and oranges of pyracantha berries take the autumn garden through to winter as silver-misted spiders webs adorn the evergreen stems.

such as ground elder, bindweed and couch grass there are few viable alternatives. A herbicide based on Glyphosphate should be effective.

When you have killed off weeds the soil should be double dug, in trenches. Take out two spits (two spade depths) of soil and lay it aside on a sheet of plastic, until you have completed the first trench. Dig another line next to the first trench (two spits deep again) and put that soil into the first empty trench. Continue along the length of the border filling the last trench with the first spits of soil you removed. Incorporate as much bulky compost and manure as possible at the lowest level. The ice and frosts of winter will break up the large lumps of soil into a fine tilth for planting in spring.

Established beds and borders can be forked over or, if you prefer, mulched with compost. Mulching is best carried out in mid winter when earlier rains should have thoroughly wetted the soil. Mulching both feeds the plant and keeps down the weeds. Mulch cannot easily be penetrated by rainwater so it is best to mulch when the soil is wet. Although the mulch is only on the surface it is where most plants feed with their surface roots and will eventually be carried down to a lower level to be ready for the new burst of growth in spring. Gardens that suffer from dry summers, chalk or heavy clay require considerable quantities of mulch.

After a winter frost, always look over plants to check they have not been lifted by the freezing action. If any have, cut the plant down, split it, replant it and mulch it in one go as too much working on wet ground compacts and damages the soil.

Winter is the time to cut down all the herbaceous perennials that turn into woody sticks, trim back the evergreen edgers and cut growths of climbers. Much of this can be used for your compost. This is also the time to prune shrubs. *Buddleia davidii* can be cut hard back now as it is extremely tough. Cuttings placed at the back of the border will make new plants. It is often advised that philadelphus, deutzias and spirea are pruned after they flower. However, they are often easier to deal with in winter. Study the bare bush carefully to find all the shoots that flowered the previous season – they will be twiggy, sometimes with dried flowers still attached. New growth will be smooth, greener and unbranched. Cut the old growth back to the new stems arising along it. Then feed and mulch. Roses are best pruned between early and late winter. Whole books have been written about how and when to prune roses. However, there are a few simple rules that can be followed: cut shrub roses only when they get overgrown, whereas modern cluster-flowered and old hybrid tea roses need to be pruned back to about 45cm (18ins), always to an outfacing bud. They must then be heavily fed to compensate for such butchery. Some people advocate the simple but brutal method of cutting straight through rose bushes with hedging shears to the height you want them. They will flower as well as with any other method, but a lot of dead, twiggy growth will be left in the centre, which is difficult to remove.

Shrubs such as lavender (*Lavandula* spp.), santolina, rue (*Ruta graveolens*), and rosemary (*Rosmarinus*) should be sheared to compact domes in late winter. They

Yellow and orange crown Imperilas *are complemented perfectly by* Fritillaria Verticillata *to make a lush-looking border.*

may look bare for a couple of weeks but they soon make fresh growth. In very cold climates wait until the weather is milder before cutting back as frost may get into the cuts and damage soft growth.

Many herbaceous plants flower well only if they are divided every three years, and this task is best carried out in late winter, just as you feel the soil and plants are getting ready for a surge of growth. Plants to divide include asters, which spread fast unless they are frequently divided, and geraniums, which make huge clumps which might overwhelm finer plants. With geraniums dig up the plant and, using two forks back to back, prise it apart. The clump can be split further to make several new plants.

APPENDIX I

TREES, SHRUBS, PERENNIALS AND BULBS FOR SPRING COLOUR

Trees

Amelanchier lamarckii – masses of tiny white flowers over bronze new leaves.

Cercis siliquastrum – bright pink flowers, heart-shaped leaves.

Cydonia oblonga (true quince) – large leaves, huge, white, single flowers.

Malus floribunda – covered in pink and white blossom. Some *Malus* cultivars have white or pink blossom.

Mespilus germanica (medlar) – single white flowers.

Prunus (Japanese cherry) – not at all suitable for flower beds and borders, but *P.* 'Taihaku', with its lovely white flowers is irresistible.

Shrubs

Azalea and *Rhododendron* – numerous cultivars, ranging from tiny to large with good foliage in shape, colour and size. This is one of the most versatile plant families, but it needs acid soil and high rainfall.

Camellia – all do best on acid soil with high rainfall, but will adapt to border life.

Forsythia – the bright yellow flowers the hallmark of spring; *F.* × *intermedia* 'Lynwood' and *F.* 'Beatrix Farrand' are spectacular.

Magnolia – *M.* × *loebneri* 'Leonard Messel' has lilac-pink flowers in great profusion on a tall shrub; *M.* × *loebneri* 'Merrill' is a white-flowered version of *M.* × *loebneri* and just as beautiful; *M.* × *soulangeana* bears white, chalice-shaped flowers, stained rose purple at the base, sometimes pure white, sometimes purple; *M. stellata*, the hardiest and easiest of the magnolias, has fragrant, star-shaped flowers.

Osmanthus – × *O. burkwoodii* has fragrant white flowers, starred all over a neat evergreen shrub, which can be clipped, after flowering to a neat dome; *O. delavayi* bears white, sweetly scented flowers on arching branches.

Pieris floribunda – excellent evergreen shrubs with strange new leaf growths like red flowers and panicles of white, urn-shaped flowers.

Ribes sanguineum (flowering currant) – drooping flowers, in red, pink or white; yellow cultivars are scented.

Spiraea 'Arguta' (syn. *S.* × *arguta* 'Bridal wreath') – slender, arching shoots laden with small dense clusters of white flowers.

Viburnum – *V. carlesii* is an evergreen, wide-spreading shrub with scented, pale pink flowers; *V.* × *juddii* is similar but less tall, with highly scented, pink-tinted white flowers.

Perennials

Bergenia – huge evergreen leaves support strong flowers in deep red, pink and white; one of the best perennials for beds and borders.

Brunnera macrophylla (Siberian bugloss) – large heart-shaped leaves, china blue flowers; *B. macrophylla* 'Variegata' has boldly variegated leaves, which can turn to plain, blue flowers; *B. macrophylla* 'Hadspen Cream' needs shade.

Corydalis flexuosa – a new perennial, fashionable, with bright blue flowers over ferny foliage.

Dicentra – finely cut, ferny foliage in greens, pewters and almost blue; pink and white flowers held well over the attractive foliage. *D. spectabilis* bears pink and white lockets over large ferny leaves; *D. spectabilis* var. *alba* has pure white flowers on arching stems.

Epimedium – most have shining, evergreen leaves and pale yellow flowers. Cut back in winter to show the flowers. *E.* × *youngianum* 'Niveum' has heart-shaped milk-chocolate coloured leaves in spring, white, starry flowers hover above; *E.* × *rubrum* has tinted leaves and rose-coloured flowers.

Erysimum – *E. cheiri* 'Bloody Warrior' is a deep red form of the perennial wallflower; *E. linifolium* 'Variegatum' has variegated leaves and pale mauve flowers; *E.* 'Moonlight' has pale yellow flowers; *E.* 'Rufus' has orange flowers.

Euphorbia – *E. myrsinites* has curled stems bearing almost blue leaves and terminal lime green flowers; *E. polychroma* bears mounds of bright yellow flowers over linear green foliage.

Gallium odoratum (syn. *Asperula odorata*) (sweet woodruff) – delicate, whorled foliage, tiny starred white flowers.

Omphalodes verna – heart-shaped leaves spring out as the tiny blue or white flowers unfold; good in shade as ground cover.

Pachyphragma macrophyllum – rounded foliage, umbellated white flowers.

Primula – *P. vulgaris*, the common primrose, has masses of pale yellow flowers and is good under shrubs; *P.* 'Wanda' has dark purple flowers. There are many named cultivars, with double or single flowers.

Pulmonaria (spotted dog, lungwort) – lovely in shade, the leaves are often blotched, sometimes entirely silver; blue, pink and white flowers.

Viola – the sweet violet, *V. odorata*, has pink, white and purple flowers. Cultivars include *V.* 'Columbine' with veined blue flowers, *V.* 'Moonlight' with pale cream flowers, and *V.* 'Bronwen' with blue and white flowers.

Bulbs

Anemone – *A. blanda* (windflower) has tiny ferny leaves and masses of blue, white and pink flowers; *A. nemorosa* (wood anemone) is vigorous and carpeting, masses of star-shaped flowers.

Chionodoxa (glory of the snow) – good for making sheets of strong blue under trees and shrubs; *C. forbesii* 'Pink Giant' has bright pink flowers in late spring.

Crocus – *C. chrysanthus* cultivars are very early flowering in shades of blue, cream, yellow and purple; *C. tommasinianus* is a silvery-lilac species that sometimes blooms before the spring arrives, seeds into lovely sheets; *C. vernus* has given rise to large-flowered

cultivars with lovely deep cups that stand up to bad weather in purple, deep yellow, blue and striped variations to make carpets of colour under shrubs.

Erythronium – the hybrid 'Pagoda' is ideal for shade under trees; large leaves, with dangling, bell flowers in yellow.

Fritillaria – *F. imperialis* (crown imperial) has tall, strong stems with glossy, green ruffs round pendulous buds opening to yellow, orange and coppery-red flowers; *F. meleagris* has lovely hanging purple and white chequered bells; *F. pallidiflora*, *F. pontica* and *F. pyrenaica* have subtle yellow-green flower bells.

Muscari – *M. armeniacum* has bright blue spikes of flower, too prolific for most flower beds, but an indispensable blue in late spring; *M. comosum* 'Plumosum' (feather hyacinth) has exploded spikes of violet flower; *M. latifolium* with broad leaves encircling dual-toned flowers, light blue top, violet bottom.

Narcissus – a huge range to choose from. The large ones have strong foliage, which can be difficult to cope with. Miniatures are better, with *N.* 'Tête-à-Tête' one of the best yellows and *N.* 'Thalia' a multi-flowered white.

Tulipa – there are hundreds of species and varieties, making it one of the best subjects for a mixed bed or border.

APPENDIX II

SHRUBS, PERENNIALS AND BULBS FOR SUMMER COLOUR

Shrubs

Buddleia davidii – there are many named forms, with spires of flower in colours ranging from white to darkest purple. *B. davidii* 'Dartmoor' is more elegant than most, with multi-panicles of blue flower.

Ceanothus – bright blue blossom on evergreen shrubs, which do best with some protection. *C. thyrsiflorus* var. *repens* makes a mounded shrub, which is hardy and reliably blue in early summer.

Cistus – evergreen, often spicily-scented leaves of many shapes, colours and textures; all have papery flowers in shades of white through to deepest carmine, and they flower prodigiously in midsummer. They need a dry, sheltered spot.

Clematis – can be used to twine into trees and shrubs. Best are the *viticella* hybrids, particularly *C. viticella* 'Etoile Violette' and *C. viticella* 'Purpurea Plena Elegans'; herbaceous clematis include *C. integrifolia* in white, pink or mauve which is a good border plant; *C. recta* with clouds of tiny white flowers. All should be pruned to near ground level in early spring.

Deutzia – beautiful shrubs grown for their prolific flowers in early to midsummer. Spectacular cascading pink and white blossom. *D.* × *elegantissima* 'Rosealind' and *D.* × *hybrida* 'Magicien' are very fine.

Exochorda racemosa – abundant, snowy white flowers.

Hypericum – *H.* 'Hidcote' is a tall, evergreen shrub, smothered nearly all summer in yellow, saucer-shaped flowers; *H. kouytchense* is a graceful, arching shrub, loaded with flowers and exotic seedheads.

Kolkwitzia amabilis (beauty bush) – tall, wide-spreading shrub with tiny, furry leaves; pink flowers cascade along the arching branches.

Lavatera – *L.* 'Barnsley' is a large shrub covered with pale pink, pink-eyed flowers from midsummer to the first frosts; *L. thuringiaca* 'Ice Cool' is smaller with more upright growth but less spectacular, though equally long-lasting, white flowers.

Philadelphus – large shrubs, with miraculous scented blossom for a few weeks in early summer. Many beautiful named varieties with single or double white flowers, some tinted with purple. *P. coronarius* 'Aureus' is border worthy for its golden-yellow foliage in early spring, starred with white flowers in summer. Plant it in shade; avoid sun.

Syringa (lilac) – many varieties; deep purple, mauve and white forms proliferate. *Syringa* × *josiflexa* 'Bellicent' is a smaller shrub with deep pink flowers; *S. meyeri* 'Palibin' is small, only 1.5m (5ft) after many years, covered with tiny tubular pinky-mauve scented flowers, sometimes twice in a season.

Viburnum plicatum 'Mariesii' – tiered and spreading branches layered with flat, white flowers.

Weigela – *W.* 'Florida Variegata' has lovely cream and green foliage to set off the clusters of pink flowers; *W. middendorffiana* is a slow-growing species with tubular yellow flowers; *W.* 'Candida' has pure white flowers.

Perennials

Achillea – ferny foliage, pink, white, red and salmon, flat flowerheads. *A.* 'Moonshine' has silver foliage, flat, bright yellow flowers.

Alchemilla mollis – mound-forming with velvety, scalloped leaves and sheaves of lime green flowers.

Anthemis – *A. cupaniana* has silver grey thread-like foliage, white daisy flowers; *A. tinctoria* 'E.C. Buxton' has ferny foliage, masses of long-lasting, yellow daisy flowers.

Campanula – many named cultivars with spotted flowers or showers of blue and white ones. *C. lactiflora* cultivars are tall, with heads of light blue, white or pink flowers; *C. latiloba* and *C. latiloba* var. *alba* bear tall spikes of, respectively, blue-grey and white flowers; *C. persicifola* has little white or blue Canterbury bells all up the stems.

Centaurea – all have good, silvery, palmate leaves and shaggy flowers in pink, blue and white. *C.* 'Pulchra Major' has large grey leaves, huge scaly buds opening to cyclamen-pink flowers.

Coreopsis – *C.* 'Moonbeam' has delicate, thread-like leaves, surmounted with fragile pale yellow daisies, and makes a cloud effect at the front of a border; *C.* 'Zagreb' is much more substantial.

Crambe cordifolia – immense cabbagy leaves, 1.8m (6ft) tall, branching heads of white flowers.

Dianthus – the famous old 'pink'. All have fine, silver-grey foliage and scented carnation-like flowers in white, pink or red, many edged, blotched and marbled with dark colours.

Delphinium – tall blue, pink and white spires of bells that dominate the summer garden.

Geranium – hardy, tough plants in hundreds of species and varieties. Best blues include *G.* 'Johnson's Blue', *G.* × *magnificum*, *G.* 'Brookside'; whites include, *G. clarkei* 'Kashmir White' and some of the *G. sylvaticum* forms for shade; among the pinks, *G.* × *oxonianum* 'Wargrave Pink' is prolific.

Gypsophila paniculata – up to 90cm (3ft) tall, but airy, threading tiny stems with tiny white or pink stars.

Helenium – rich yellow, brown-red, copper and orange flowers in late summer.

Hemerocallis (day lilies) – spectacular trumpet-shaped flowers in many colours. *H. fulva* is an old yellow variety; *H.* 'Catherine Woodbery', a modern hybrid, has blush-pink flowers.

Hosta – a large selection of indispensable perennials. Smaller varieties have interesting striped and shaded leaves. Mostly grown for foliage interest, all have flowers in white or lilac.

Iris – sword-shaped foliage on the massive border irises; the smaller standard dwarf bearded and miniature bearded iris are numerous and have an exciting colour range; *I.* 'Gingerbread Man' has brown flowers with a vivid blue beard; *I.* 'Jade Mist' has smoked green standards and chartreuse spotted blue beard. *I. sibirica* cultivars have grassy leaves, smaller flowers, and 'Flight of Butterflies' is an apt description of the type.

Knautia macedonica – basal groups of palmate leaves, dark red, scabious-like flowers on fine stems.

Kniphofia – dramatic, spiky foliage, flower spikes in red, orange, yellow, apricot, cream, white and green.

Lysimachia – *L. ephemerum* has useful tall, white spikes of flower in late summer; *L. clethroides* has creamy-white spires of small cupped flowers; *L. ciliata* has bronzed foliage and yellow flowers. All like moist soil.

Lythrum – tall, dramatic perennials for back of border. *L. salicaria* 'Firecandle' has huge spires of magenta flower.

Macleaya microcarpa – 'Kelway's Coral Plume' is one of the best with enormous, glaucous blue-green leaves, which always have a pink tinge to them; it is topped with sprays of small, coral pink flowers.

Monarda (bergamot) – all have spectacular hooded flowers, in colours from white to a dark mahogany through pink and blue. *M.* 'Cambridge Scarlet' is actually soft crimson.

Morina longifolia – leaves that look like a spiny thistle leaves but are soft, make clumps of shiny foliage surmounted with pink whorls of flower.

Paeonia cvs – a huge family with many named cultivars. Some are single – particularly beautiful is *P.* 'White Wings' – others are double – *P.* 'Sarah Bernhardt' is a good example of a sumptuous pink and white beauty. The species – including *P. mlokosewitschii* – and tree forms are easy and useful in mixed borders.

Papaver – *P. orientale* is particularly good in beds and borders, with a wonderful colour range, except for blue, and easy to grow and overplant with annuals once the poppies have faded; *P. heldreichii* is a lovely soft apricot poppy; *P. somniferum* is the annual opium poppy, with silvery leaves and buds opening to huge single or double heads.

Penstemon – *P.* 'Garnet' is one of the hardiest cultivars, with deep ruby flowers. Again

there is every colour from white, through pink and red to blues and the darkest of all that include *P.* 'Merlin', *P.* 'Blackbird' and *P.* 'Russian River'.

Phlox paniculata – indispensable plants for the late summer border, with rounded heads of flowers in clear, pretty colours. Need moisture.

Salvia – a large genus of border plants, with new ones continually introduced, many collected in America. *S. nemorosa* 'East Friesland' is a good dark blue clumper; *S. patens* is a nearly hardy bright blue flowerer; *S. × sylvestris* 'Rose Queen' has bright rose pink flowers.

Selinum wallichianum (syn. *S. tenuifolium*) – mounding ferny leaves support delicate heads of white flower.

Strobilanthes atropurpureus – woody, furred stems loaded with inky blue flowers.

Thalictrum – tall, graceful with foliage similar to aquilegia; lovely sprays of violet, mauve and white flowers carried at about 1m (3ft).

Bulbs

Allium ssp. – many species and some new cultivars, some invasive, but all beautiful in shades of dark red, pink, blue, yellow and white. *A. aflatunense* bears tall drumsticks of blue flowers; *A. caeruleum* (syn. *A. azureum*) has bright blue balls on wiry stems; *A.*

christophii (syn. *A. albopilosum*) has enormous balls of silver-mauve flowers.

Crocosmia – *C.* 'Citronella' has lovely soft yellow flowers, sword-shaped leaves; *C.* 'Lucifer' has tall stems of flame-red flowers, sword-shaped leaves; *C.* 'Solfaterre' has soft apricot flowers over bronzed leaves.

Galtonia – *G. candicans* (summer hyacinth) has elegant spires of white bells; *G. viridiflora* – spikes of white-green flowers, grey-green leaves. Bulbs planted in spring establish easily in the right conditions.

Lilium – an enormous range of species and cultivars, most of which prefer acid soil, especially *L. speciosum*. *L. canadense*, the Madonna lily, will tolerate some lime, as will *L. henryi*, a magnificent orange, *L. regale*, the best white, and the tiger lily, *L. tigrinum*. Some of the hardier hybrids are easy: *L.* 'Connecticut King', a bright yellow that quickly forms clumps; *L.* 'Pink Perfection'; *L.* 'African Queen', a soft apricot; and the Citronella strain, which will grow into magnificent large groups in well-drained soil. All prefer good drainage, but even in ideal conditions it is rare for them to last for more than a few years in the ground.

TREES, SHRUBS, PERENNIALS, BULBS AND GRASSES FOR AUTUMN COLOUR

Trees

Acers – leaves of most species and cultivars become red and yellow.

Koelreuteria paniculata (golden rain tree, pride of India) – huge panicles of yellow flowers in autumn followed by large seed pods and bright yellow leaves.

Malus – cultivars include 'Golden Hornet', 'John Downie', 'Red Jade' and 'Red Sentinel'; one of the best genus of trees for autumn fruits, golden yellow, pink and red.

Sorbus – *S. cashmiriana*, *S. hupehensis* and *S. vilmorinii* are good for autumn leaf colour, with scarlet, yellow, pink and white berries.

Shrubs

Bupleurum fruticosum – jade green evergreen leaves, at their best with bright yellow panicles of flowers in early autumn.

Caryopteris – graceful, small, arched ever-grey shrub, laced with vibrant blue flowers.

Ceratostigma – *C. griffithii* and *C. willmottianum* have rich blue flowers in early autumn; leaves turn red in autumn; cut down in spring for best flowers.

Clerodendrum – *C. bungei* is a semi-woody, suckering shrub, with large dark leaves and large corymbs of pink flowers in early autumn; *C. trichotomum* is a large shrub with white, maroon-cupped, fragrant flowers followed by bright blue berries.

Cornus – *C. alternifolia* 'Argentea' a layered variety, with tiny puckered and crimped variegated leaves; *C. controversa* 'Variegata' is a lovely layered shrub with tiered branches loaded with white-edged leaves, especially dramatic-looking in autumn.

Cotoneaster – a large genus of deciduous and evergreen shrubs, varying in size from ground-hugging tinies to ones that take on tree-like proportions; all have red or yellow fruits in autumn.

Euonymus – *E. alatus*, *E. planipes* (syn. *E. sachalinensis*) have large scarlet fruits, red leaf colour, interesting branches; *E. europeus* 'Red Cascade' has pendulous branches, weighed down with red fruit.

Hydrangea – *H. macrophylla* 'Ayesha' has china blue flowers fading to sea green; *H.* 'Preziosa' has dark pink flowers ageing to deep ruby.

Nandina domestica (Chinese sacred bamboo) – jade green stems, with delicate leaves turning a brilliant crimson; insignificant white flowers in the autumn.

Perovskia atriplicifolia 'Blue Spire' – grey foliage, white stems, intense blue flowers in spires in early autumn.

Pyracantha – grown as a shrub it makes an excellent back-of-border subject where its evergreen leaves make a good background; good white flowers in early summer, but huge panicles of yellow, orange or bright red berries are spectacular.

Rosa – *R.* 'Iceberg' is one of the best for autumn flowers, bearing clusters of pure white almost until Christmas; *R. rugosa* 'Alba' has white single flowers, scarlet hips, leaves turn pale yellow; *R. rugosa* 'Frau Dagmar Hastrup' has pink single flowers, huge red hips.

Yucca gloriosa – dramatic spiked foliage, sometimes striped in yellow or white.

Perennials

Aconitum – *A. carmichaelii* – tall growing, dark green leaves, deep blue flowers; *A. carmichaelii* 'Kelmscott' has tall spikes of pale blue flowers; *A.* 'Sparks Variety' tall dark blue flowers.

Anemone × *hybrida* (Japanese anemone) – vine-shaped leaves, tall, gleaming, cup-shaped flowers, single and double, in pink, white and red colours.

Artemisia lactiflora – dark jagged leaves and spires of white flowers; *A. lactiflora* Guizho Group has astonishing black leaved version of above with almost the same dramatic white flowers.

Aster – *A. divaricatus* has shiny black stems topped with tiny white flowers; *A. ericoides* 'Pink Cloud' is a billowing mass of pink from early autumn until frost; *A.* × *frikartii* 'Mönch' has large lavender blue flowers; *A. lateriflorus* 'Horizontalis' a strong grower with fan-like branches, massed with white, pink-centred flowers;

A. novae-angliae 'Alma Potschke' and 'Harrison's Pink' have, respectively, spectacular cerise and pale pink, no mildew, good foliage colour; *A. pringlei* 'Monte Cassino' has clouds of tiny white flowers on a strong-growing plant; *A. thomsonii* 'Nanus' long-petalled, lilac flowers over neat small plants; *A. tradescantii* has masses of white flowers, a foil for autumn colours.

Bupleurum – *B. falcatum* and *B. angulosum* have neat, narrow foliage with tall heads of lime green flowers in the autumn.

Cimicifuga simplex – 'White Pearl' are tall, graceful plants with divided foliage and plumes of white flowers; *C. simplex* 'Brunette' has dark brown leaves to show off its bottle brush flowers.

Cynara cardunculus – huge, jagged silver leaves, bright purple-blue thistle heads in early autumn.

Dahlias – hundreds of colours, shapes and sizes flowering from late summer to the first autumn frosts.

Dendranthema – *D.* 'Bronze Elegance' has bronzed clusters of chrysanthemum flowers from early autumn; *D.* 'Emperor of China' has pale pink flowers over leaves that turn deep garnet.

Echinops ritro – bright blue balls of flower.

Eupatorium – *E. purpureum* is

tall, to 1.5m (5ft), red-tinged stems and leaves, heads of red-purple flowers through autumn; *E. rugosum* has panicles of white flowers on a much bushier plant, not quite so tall.

Gaura lindheimeri – thin, wiry stems that hold flowers like flights of butterflies coloured in creams and pinks; a variegated leaved variety is not so hardy.

Geranium wallichianum 'Buxton's Variety' – leaves are marked in red and stems trailing to 1.5m (5ft) each is starred with bright blue flowers.

Iris foetidissima 'Variegata' – white-striped leaves, clusters of orange seedheads; the plain-leaved variety is much more reliable in flower and fruiting.

Liriope muscari – grassy leaves, with spikes of blue or white flowers.

Malva sylvestris 'Primley Blue' – bright blue flowers over sprawling stems.

Ophiopogon planiscapus 'Nigrescens' – jet black grassy leaves.

Origanum laevigatum 'Herrenhausen' – long sprays of purple flowers.

Salvia – *S. patens* has gentian blue hooded flowers, but not reliably hardy; *S. uliginosa* is a tall, blue flower suitable for the back of borders where its colour shines among late white roses.

Sedum S. spectabile or *S.*

'Autumn Joy' glaucous fleshy leaves, coral pink, flat flower heads loved by butterflies; *S. spurium* 'Atropurpureum' has dark purple leaves and wine red flowers; *S. telephium* 'Variegatum' has almost white leaves mottled with pale green, with pink flower heads.

Strobilanthes atropurpureus – hairy stems, with ink blue flowers.

Symphytum × uplandicum 'Variegata' – large leaves with creamy white margins. New growth in autumn.

Verbena bonariensis – square, upright stems with massed, tiny, purplish flower heads.

Bulbs

Colchicums – amazing pink and white flowers through bare earth in autumn.

Crocus autumnalis – blue, purple and white crocus flowers.

Cyclamen hederifolium – tiny pink or white flowers over marbled leaves.

Nerine bowdenii – strap-shaped leaves, shocking pink showers of flower; some white varieties.

Grasses

Alopecurus pratensis 'Aureus' – striking low clumps, vividly striped in green and gold.

Carex oskimensis 'Evergold' – neat mounds of striped green and white grass.

Cortaderia (pampas grass) – lovely as isolated specimen, good with other grasses; huge plumes of feathery flowers; *C. selloana* 'Gold Band' and 'Albolineata' are variegated versions.

Deschampsia (hairgrasses) – luxuriant 60–90cm (2–3ft) high, airy-looking, golden flower heads.

Elymus magellanicum (syn. *Agropyron magellanicum*) (blue wheat grass) – telling against autumn colour.

Hakonechloa macra 'Aureola' (golden satin grass) – delicate streaks of green over gold, turns bronze in winter.

Helictotrichon sempervirens – hemisphere of pale blue-coloured grasses.

Melica altissima 'Atropurpurea' – elegant grass with purple silky seedheads.

Miscanthus – *M. sinensis* var. *purparescens* has purple flower stalks, silver flower plumes; *M. sinensis* 'Silberfeder' a green grass fountain with silver grass heads; *M. sinensis* 'Variegatus' a spectacular grass growing tall and straight, with blades of grass strikingly variegated in cream.

Stipa – *S. gigantea* fountains of shining green leaves with massive heads of oats; *S. tenuissima* has feathery flower spikes, which bleach to cream in autumn.

APPENDIX IV

TREES, SHRUBS, PERENNIALS AND BULBS FOR WINTER INTEREST

Trees

Arbutus − *A. unedo* a small evergreen tree with flowers and 'strawberry' fruit at the same time; *A.* × *andrachnoides* has exciting cinnamon-coloured bark as well as good evergreen leaves and flowers.

Acers − *A. davidii, A. grosseri, A. pensylvanicum* and *A. rufinerve* are small trees with beautifully striped trunk and stems; *A. griseum* (paperbark maple) has flaking and curling bark that reveals polished cinnamon-coloured trunk beneath, good autumn colour; *A. palmatum* 'Senkaki' (coral bark maple), all branches and trunk are a magnificent coral red colour all the year round, good pink leaves in spring and autumn.

Betula (birch) − *B. albosinensis* var. *septentronalis* has shining orange-brown bark with pink and grey shading; *B. ermanii* has pinkish-white bark; *B. jaquemontii, B. papyrifera* and *B. pendula* have gleaming white bark, delicate twig tracery against winter sky.

Cupresses arizonica var. *glabra* − blue conifer in silver-grey, lovely cones.

Ilex (holly) − *I. altaclerensis* 'Golden King' has bright gold and green foliage and red berries; *I. altaclerensis* 'Lawsoniana' is nearly spineless with shaded olive green and yellow leaves; *I. aquifolium* 'Handsworth New Silver' has purple stems, green mottled grey leaves with a broad silver margin; *I. crenata* 'Shiro-fukurin' and *I. myrtifolia* are lovely small-leaved hollies, narrow and small habit.

Phillyrea angustifolia − good dark evergreen for clipping.

Prunus − *P. serrula* has bark which bears a strong resemblance to dark red ribbons; *P.* × *subhirtella* 'Autumnalis' bears clusters of pretty white or pink flowers from late autumn to spring.

Taxus baccata 'Fastigiata' − green forms are excellent for winter architecture; *T. baccata* 'Fastigiata Aurea' makes bright golden exclamation marks of strong colour in beds and borders.

Shrubs

Buxus − large genus of excellent evergreen for winter furniture, clipped as balls or as free-growing shrub, many varieties with gold leaves.

Cornus − *C. alba* a species of vigorous deciduous shrubs with coloured stems; *C. mas* 'Variegata' has tiny yellow flowers in late winter and variegated leaves in spring and summer.

Danae racemosa (Alexandrian laurel) − glossy evergreen leaves on a graceful arched shrub.

Daphne − *D. bholua* 'Gurkha' has large, reddish-mauve buds, opening to white, purple flushed flowers in late winter to early spring; *D. mezereum* bears sweet-scented purple or white flowers in early spring; *D. odora* 'Aureomarginata' has white variegated leaves, scented pink flowers appear in late winter.

Euonymus fortunei 'Silver Queen' − eventually becomes a large domed shrub of startling white and green foliage.

Fatsia japonica – huge, evergreen, palmate, polished leaves, the interesting combination of white flowers and black berries appears in winter.

Garrya elliptica 'James Roof'; – long, grey-green 'catkins' in winter, evergreen leaves.

Hamamelis (witch hazel) – *H.* × *intermedia* 'Jelena' bears red, scented flowers in late winter to early spring; other cultivars have copper, bronze or bright yellow flowers; 'Pallida' has pale primrose flowers strongly scented in large clusters.

Hedera colchica 'Sulphur Heart' (syn. 'Paddy's Pride') (ivy) – variegated cultivar for ground cover and on pillars.

Jasmine nudiflorum (winter jasmine) – bright yellow, scented flowers on leafless emerald green stems to climb on fences and trellises and provide good ground cover.

Mahonia – *M. aquifolium*, *M. japonica* Bealei Group and *M.* × *media* 'Charity' are striking evergreen shrubs with whorls of leaves and yellow, scented flowers.

Sarcococca – *S. confusa* and *S. hookeriana* var. *dignya* are small, shining evergreen shrubs with intensely perfumed winter flowers.

Viburnum – *V.* × *bodnantense* 'Dawn' is a tall, rangy deciduous shrub, best pink winter flowers, highly scented; *V. tinus* (Laurustinus) has good evergreen foliage, clustered pink and white flowers appear from late autumn through to early spring.

Perennials

Arum italicum ssp. *italicum* 'Marmoratum' (syn. *A.i.* var. *pictum*) – marbled leaves in winter, red poker seedheads.

Erica – a huge genus of subshrubs for hardy winter borders.

Euphorbia – *E. characias* ssp. *wulfenii* is a large, shrub-like plant with tall grey-green stems to make an architectural feature in winter border, and huge heads of lime green flowers in late winter; *E. robbiae* has whorls of evergreen foliage at ground level with olive green flowers, an excellent, hardy plant for ground cover under shrubs.

Helleborus – *H. argutifolius*, *H. foetidus*, *H. niger* and *H. orientalis* have lovely jagged evergreen leaves, starred with flowers in green, cream, pink, purple and black; there are also some spotted forms.

Iris – *I. foetidissima* has sword-shaped, evergreen leaves with tiny mauve or yellow flowers in spring, winter interest in foliage and seedheads in bright orange; *I. histriodes* 'Major' – intense blue tiny iris needs a sheltered spot for very early flowers; *I. reticulata* 'Katharine Hodgkin' is early flowering with blue-suffused yellow flowers; *I. unguicularis* (syn. *I. stylosa*) blue or white flowers in midwinter, sweetly scented.

Vinca (periwinkle) – good, if invasive, evergreen trailing foliage, some are heavily variegated, with blue, white and mauve flowers in the late winter.

Bulbs

Cyclamen coum – heart-shaped, silver patterned leaves, lots of carmine flowers.

Eranthis hyemalis (winter aconite) – deep golden, cup-shaped flowers which are rather like buttercups over ruffed curled foliage.

Galanthus – large genus, some single, some double flowers, petals green-edged, yellow centres; some tall, some minute; *G. nivalis* (common snowdrop) – single, prolific, tiny white bells over narrow, grass-like foliage.

INDEX

Page numbers in *italic* refer to illustrations